GEORDIEFELLA
ROAD TO HELL

TAGL PUBLISHING

Published by
TAGL Publishing
Newcastle upon Tyne, England.

First published in Great Britain
by TAGL Publishing 2006

ISBN 0-9554355-0-1
ISBN 978-0-9554355-0-8

Printed in Great Britain by Athenaeum Press Ltd
Gateshead, Tyne & Wear

Cover Design and Book Layout
by John McGibbon

ACKNOWLEDGEMENT

I would like to thank my family, Linda, Anthony, Graeme and Julie for the support they have given me over the last twenty years.
This dream would not have been possible without the confidence shown in me by Gary Rhodes and Granada Television to whom I am eternally grateful.
And finally a special thanks to Senty, Becka, Laura and Riffi, who all believed in me throughout Hell's Kitchen.

Terry Miller.

This book was a joy to work on. Over a long period of time I have been privileged to become friends with Terry while researching and preparing this book for him and I would like to thank him and his entire family who welcomed me into their circle. I'm proud to say they are my friends.
To my wife Lynda and daughter Lesley, I would like to add my love and appreciation. Throughout the writing of the book they supported me unstintingly and provided me with the endless cups of tea I asked for.

Gordon Taylor.

CONTENTS

Contents

FOREWORD

I've known Terry for quite a while now and have had the opportunity to get to know him well over the months. We've shared a beer together and visited the races and I'm delighted that he is doing so well.

He's the kind of hard working Geordie lad who represents the North East well and his food is out of this world.

I wish him the best of luck with the autobiography and hope it will be a great success.

Alan Shearer.

CHAPTER ONE

IN A NUTSHELL

F ood critics are a strange breed of people, many of them are professional in their outlook and competent in their approach towards an honest and fair assessment of a chef's food, others are anything but honest and fair.

My one concern about the reports they publish is the fact that, having visited a restaurant once, they may give it a non committal or poor report when the fact is that it could be an off day. We're all human, everyone has them.

I honestly believe that a critic should visit any food establishment a minimum of three times before preparing a report on the fare on offer, one bad report can be a disaster and even lead to the closure of the restaurant. Food critics should at least give the establishment a fair crack of the whip.

One of my bugbears is a critic appearing unannounced in the restaurant and not giving me the chance to prepare my best work. In fact I wish they wouldn't appear at all, it would be miles better if they visited the local greasy spoon where there are real food problems to contend with.

It never ceases to amaze me how the general public will read newspapers or watch T.V. and accept a critic's advice on a chef's cooking when most of the critics have never attempted to produce a dish or have any talent for cooking in general. We're all different as it says in Monty Python's Life of Brian and that's true about food as in anything else.

We all have different likes and dislikes and what I find tasty, you might not, so the motto I would give you is 'TRY IT YOURSELF ?' If you don't like it you don't have to go back but for God's sake, make your own judgement.

I've deliberately gone down the road of making this book a good account of what I'm about as a bloke with a hint of controversy along the way. I'll tell you about growing up on council estates which were famed for their mob culture, the highs and lows I've experienced in twenty years of the hospitality industry, my horse racing experiences with Pride of Pendle, my filly which has given me so much pleasure, my family and plenty of other varied experiences including Hell's Kitchen. It wont all be pretty but I hope it will be eye opening.

Through my success in Hell's Kitchen, I am now in the lucky position of running my own restaurant, am happily married to Linda and have some great family in my sons, Anthony and Graeme, and my step daughter, Julie. It doesn't get much better than this in life and all of them have been solidly behind me over the years.

Going down the road is a good way to start as I spent many years in road gangs, laying Tarmac and the heat of that is similar to the heat of the kitchen. It's bloody uncomfortable but it has its rewards at the end of the job.

I wouldn't have missed laying the black stuff for a

pension but cooking is the passion of my life, along with Newcastle United, the great Geordie nation, my racehorse but most importantly, my family.

How my wife Linda has put up with me all these years is a mystery to me. She was the driving force behind me getting into and winning Hell's Kitchen. If she hadn't hoodwinked me into attending the audition, there is no way on God's earth that I would have put myself forward. It's funny how things turn out for the best in life.

We're partners in life as well as business and we've had our run-ins like most couples. The plates can fly (a little too accurately at times) when the pressure of running our restaurant in Newcastle is on, but what I would do without her I just wouldn't like to think.

Most people have skeletons in their cupboards and mine rattle away constantly. For this book I'm going to take them out and give them an airing and I make no bones about many of the problems I have had to put up with; some of my own making, some not. You can't live your life as a saint and who would want to? I certainly don't. I'm me, what you see is what you get.

I eat and drink what I'm comfortable with and when people offer me expensive Chardonnays or other wines and I turn them down in favour of a simple Piesporter, they look at me like I'm from another planet. In fact, I am a firm believer that if you like it, have it. You should be eating and drinking to please yourself and not to satisfy other people's ideas of what you should enjoy.

Between you and me, I will let you into a little secret - they often prefer my options when they taste them. That's one of the problems today, there is too much arrogance about food and drink in my view. Too many snooty individuals pontificating about it, when in reality they prefer a nice piece of North Sea Cod to that expensive Dover sole - but heaven forbid they should admit to the fact.

I know a lot of people who have suffered from heartburn by drinking dry wines and when I have suggested they try my choice, they ring me the following day to say they are converted.

I've watched many chefs working on T.V. and there are some I have a lot of time for. Gary Rhodes is a good example. He came from nowhere to take the cooking industry by storm. The man has managed to become a first rate chef without demonstrating all the prima donna characteristics which some of the others exhibit. When I appeared on Hell's Kitchen, I got to see the man first hand and I was just dumbfounded at his professionalism and natural ability. The way he puts over his knowledge is exactly how I would like to do it myself, simple and straightforward. He is a true gent in the kitchen.

On the opening night of my new restaurant, Gary turned up to open the place for me as he had promised he would. I'm sure he had a good evening and to have my two heroes in Gary and the immortal Alan Shearer on photographs with me was just absolutely awesome. I can't thank you enough lads.

Unfortunately, I can't say the same about some of the others I've worked under. The chefs' code and the legal profession forbid me to say what I think about certain individuals but I am sick and tired of watching rudeness to staff for the sake of being rude. It's not constructive in my opinion and does nothing for team spirit in the kitchen. Of course, there are times when a head chef has to be forthright and get his point across, but to belittle someone just to satisfy ego isn't my style and never will be.

It reminds me of the bullying that went on when I attended school. I hated that too. There is no need for it and if I could tell that to youngsters today, I would. Fortunately, that kind of thing didn't happen to me or my five brothers. If nothing else came from my appearance on Hell's Kitchen, I am proud of the fact that one of my friend's daughters, who was being terrorised at school, found that it all stopped when the persecutors discovered that she knew me. My popularity among the kids following the Hell's Kitchen victory was the thing that changed their attitude. I gave her a photograph of Gary Rhodes and Alan Shearer and she became one of the most popular girls in the school.

I don't want you to get the idea that I'm a saint in the kitchen because I'm not. Little things which don't go right are a particular annoyance of mine. When you have explained in detail what is required of someone and it goes wrong I can blow my top and do my fair share of bawling and screaming and it's not that I enjoy doing it, but good money being wasted really drives me insane. Money is too hard to come by, especially in the restaurant business.

When I think of my dad, who worked on the railways, emptying carriages for a living, and the family struggling to survive on his wages, you can understand why I am very careful where the wastage of money is concerned.

He died many years ago and I wonder if he would have been proud of my success on Hell's Kitchen? There are only two or three times in my life when I have cried; once when he died and then a couple of times on the show, when the pressure was on. I'll tell you a little more about that later when I discuss the whole Hell's Kitchen experience in more depth.

My mother, Catherine, did a full day's work as well as looking after her family. She worked at the Department of Health and Social Security at Longbenton in Newcastle as a cleaner and rose to be in charge of all five hundred of the cleaning staff there. In fact, she was awarded the British Empire Medal for her work and the entire family are proud of her achievement.

Through my mam and dad's direction when I was young, and their insistence that I remember my roots, I'm as unlike any of the celebrity chefs as you could get. I don't mind a bit of fun in my kitchen and I encourage it so long as it doesn't interfere with work. As long as it stops when the customers arrive and it doesn't hinder safety, then I'm happy for the staff to enjoy themselves. It boils down to attitude and I always say, a laugh a day keeps the problems away.

In my Newcastle restaurant, which I created with the winnings from Hell's Kitchen, I have ensured that the kitchen is visible to the customers. I want them to be able to see the work going on and to be able to discuss their food with me, if it's convenient. I really think more chefs should be more accessible, instead of hiding themselves behind four walls. Where is the customer satisfaction in that? What job enjoyment? I like to see the look of pleasure on a diner's face when they have enjoyed the experience and I want to be part of it all, not just ancillary to the rest of their night. I have set myself up for being shot down by other chefs by saying that but what the hell? It's my opinion and I stand by it.

You have probably realised that I like basic cooking which is well done. I can do anything that anyone asks me for but I really wish more basic and filling dishes would become popular again.

When I'm busy, I like to call out to the lads to encourage them, telling them this is real cooking, not pinging microwaves sounding all over the place. Having that personal communication (builds up) their morale and it shows on their faces. I work with people not machines.

Nouvelle cuisine for me was a waste of time when it appeared in the 80s. The portions wouldn't keep a two-year-old alive, never mind a growing man. That was a fashion driven by the industry and to me it did as much harm as good.

My main cooking ambition is to make the food I create taste as great as I possibly can. There's still a massive demand for filling foods.

When it's a cold night in Newcastle, and believe me it can get as cold as anywhere when there is a North wind blowing, I have made a simple beef stew with dumplings containing mustard and fresh sage. It flies out from the pass and I can't keep up with the amount required. It's all the beautiful, scantily clad females out for a night of partying in Newcastle and needing a substantial meal to keep them warm.

I worry about young people today. There is a lot of laziness and too much choice of fast food which stops them from cooking. That's a great shame as they are missing out on the satisfaction of preparing a meal which their friends, wives, husbands or partners could enjoy.

One of the great things about making a satisfying meal for someone is the praise they will give you when they've enjoyed it. Everybody wants compliments and there is nothing like being told you have done well. It only takes one piece of flattery about a successful dish to encourage more experimentation.

Some recent trends have brought surprising foods to the

fore. Black Pudding is a favourite as I write this book. Over the last few years, beetroot and lemon grass have also been used a lot.

Coming out of the rise in black pudding usage, we now have white pudding coming into dishes. Anyone in the North will know that these foods have been used for years and years but other regional chefs are now utilising these foods. It isn't because we believe them to be particularly nice foods, in my view it's because we have run out of new things to try and we will do anything to appear different. It is a Northern delicacy first and foremost though.

To get a break on TV for a chef, is so important and anything different is marvellous for the medium. The fame brings an audience and that audience is vital for filling your restaurant. It's so demoralising to work in an empty place and there are so many restaurants springing up, we all need to find something different to interest our diners. I used to work in London and I couldn't cope with the place. Their culture was just so different to my own Northern personality that I found it hard to fit in. It wasn't their fault, it's the way they have developed as a multi-cultural society in the city and I couldn't seem to bond or make friends. It was a lonely time for me, spending a lot of solitary time in my flat.

It's a cut-throat environment down there, with everyone vying for better positions and morale was non existent in the food industry there. Perhaps it was my North Eastern roots but I sat around in pubs or had a coffee with only myself for company. If I made eye contact with someone, they would make a point of looking away and that's hard for someone from Newcastle, where the friendliness is so obvious. Sorry, but that's the way I saw it when I worked in London.

CHAPTER TWO

A CHILD IS BORN

Where my love for food came from is a bit of a mystery, perhaps my mother started it. I was born in 1958 and when I was growing up in 60s Newcastle, most mothers had what we called a crock pot on the stove, bubbling away with some tasty and filling stew. Even today, I still recall coming in from playing in the cold to sit down to a filling meal, with a taste that was out of this world. That's the kind of thing we've lost today.

Maybe it's the stressful and busy lives we lead which has caused us to neglect ourselves where food is concerned. After a heavy day at work, who wants to cook and wash up when it's easy to just run to the fish shop or get a pizza delivery? I'm a culprit of this myself.

It's a wonder I didn't have an identity crisis when I was born. My mother already had three sons and was desperate for a daughter. As a result, every piece of clothing she bought was pink and because of the money situation, there was no way the garments could be changed.

Whenever she took me out in my pram, women would constantly ask her about her daughter. It got so bad that she eventually bit the bullet and got me some blue clothing. I still have a hankering after pink today, but don't anyone question my sexuality!

It wasn't an easy life we led. There were six brothers and a mam and dad all living in a two bedroom flat in a place called Longbenton. It was a hell of a grounding in getting on with people believe me and, although money was tight, we managed to have just enough food to live on. I have an enormous amount of respect for my mam who worked hard to feed six growing lads and, judging by the size of me now, she did a fine job.

The estate where I lived was newly built with an entrance at either end. Two pubs, the Viking and the Rocket stood near the access to the area. It was a typical Northern estate for those days, two massive fifteen-storey blocks of flats rose above a parade of shops and were surrounded by other flats in three-storey blocks of six in each building. Four hundred and forty one West Farm Avenue was my address and luckily that block still exists today, but most of the others have been torn down and replaced by private housing and a new modern style shopping complex has also gone up.

It bears no relation to the council estate I knew as a lad and I bet the community spirit is non existent today. The blocks of flats we had then had a small square of grass outside each one which would be filled on a Sunday afternoon by the residents talking throughout the summer. The blokes would go for a pint and the women would stand around, arms folded talking and watching the hordes of kids playing in the street. Neighbours in the area used to wonder why my mam didn't take on certain houses which were offered to her and which had more rooms for her boys to be comfortable in. I know it concerned her when she found out they were talking about it, but the fact was that the houses we were offered weren't in the kind of areas she wanted her family to live so she held out for her choice of neighbourhood. I don't blame her at all for wanting to do her best where we were concerned, that's what a true mam does for her kin.

The two earliest memories I have were around three years of age. First, there was the time that my mam used to give me pink aspirin when I was unwell and I got it into my head that these pills were sweets. I watched her put them away one day and managed to get at them, stuffing down a load and making myself ill.

Illness seems to have been associated with food for me. I once had the mumps, feeling really grotty with them and I was confined to the house. My brothers ran out when the ice cream man arrived and pleaded for broken wafers which he gave them for nothing. I watched as they stuffed the lot and cried my eyes out when they didn't give me any.

Memories of Longbenton are vague for me as we only lived there until I was six years old and the main ones seem to be associated with sad events. A lot of childhood bullying went on then and I suffered my fair share of that even though I was so young.

The most frightening experience concerned a next door neighbour who came to the door of his flat opposite while I was playing in the passage between our doors. He opened the door in his dressing gown, his face white as a sheet and he croaked for me to get my mother, sliding down his door until he was flat on the floor. I was very young at the time and didn't have any idea about illness and I must have just stood there looking at him for ten minutes. He went very quiet so I raced in to get my mam who asked me how long he had been like that and I told her ages. By the time the ambulance arrived the bloke was dead. She told me later that the neighbour had suffered a heart attack but it didn't mean anything to me then, I just thought he was drunk like my dad was every Saturday.

My mam's family lived in Gateshead and we never saw them in those days. Transport wasn't the same as it is today and a small trek over the Tyne then took an age, so when two of her brothers called at the house one day, I had no idea who they were. They asked me to get her as they came in, telling her that her younger brother had died and she was needed.

These sad events seem to dominate my thinking about the days we spent in Longbenton, but things got a lot better when we were offered a new house which my mother liked.

On the day we left Longbenton I helped the removal men to fill the lorry. I had never seen so big a wagon and the sheets and ropes hanging around interior slats seemed never ending to my young mind. The men allowed me to help all morning and I was looking forward to climbing into the cab like a big removal bloke for the journey to our new house, but my dad had different ideas. He told me to join him in walking to the new area and we set off about an hour before the removal men finished the job of filling the van. Even though I was annoyed at missing the trip in the removals wagon, I remember that walk with my dad like it was yesterday. As we trudged along and talked, he pointed out the new school I was going to, Cragside Infants, and showed me landmarks along the way.

Food seems to have been a constant theme through my life because I remember moving to the new house on the day of the 1966 World Cup final. It was a huge home, much bigger than the flat we had lived in previously and the garden was full of rhubarb. Of course being me, I decided to snap it all off and eat as much as possible and even though we dipped it in sugar, I can still feel the pains of eating that straight from the garden and they were excruciating. It wasn't the best introduction to food.

There was a tree in that garden and when you climbed it you could see into the window and that's where I watched England beat Germany, perched like a sparrow in the branches.

In the main, I had a great childhood and got up to the usual tricks that most young boys do. I'm sure that I caused friends and neighbours problems on occasion but most of what I did then was just a bit of fun.

The area we had moved to is called High Heaton. It was a nice council estate, where the houses were built close together and the people always seemed to get along. If someone had a problem, the neighbours could be relied on to rally around and help, no matter how much time or effort was needed. It was the days of true community spirit, which still exists today in some places, but it doesn't seem to be like it used to be.

In those days, I could name every family on the estate and every one of their dogs too. Everyone watched each others' kids while they were playing, so they seemed to be a lot safer than today. It's sad that those kinds of concerns seem to have gone out of the community. If it came back we would all be a lot happier I'm sure.

I was full of bounce as a kid and loved every minute of my young life. Most people were playing football in Newcastle, pretending to be Wyn Davies or Pop Robson but I used to like playing cricket. There was a school called Ravenswood close to where I lived and they used to allow the local children access for playing. My brothers and friends, Philly, Stam, Whiz and the Finches used to join me in some great cricket games there, but I doubt if the M.C.C. would change their rules to allow the twenty-odd a-side matches we used to have.

In those great days you would spend hours just playing. School holidays would see kids out from 9 o'clock in the morning to the moment it got dark with maybe just a quick dinner pushed down as fast as possible to let you get back to the important business of playing.

Children seem to be looked after much better these days, probably because parents of my generation want to give them everything that we never had. The clothes and the presents we provide for them make us content that we are doing the best we can for our kids and I am one of the biggest offenders where giving is concerned. It's understandable when you consider just how poor we were when I was growing up. Mothers and grandparents are even bigger culprits but we live in the must have generation and none of us seem to be able to say no when our kids ask for things. The frightening thing for me today is how much junk food these children live on, it really pisses me off. I presented some certificates recently for mothers on a Sure Start programme, where the parents had been giving their kids a very early start on healthy eating and that was a joy to do. To see kids eating strawberries and general fruit instead of chocolate or crisps was so gratifying and the health benefits for that generation will be immense if that kind of positive action is continued and built on throughout the UK. A good blend of nutritious fare alongside 10% more exercise will help these youngsters so much.

If we can just address the problems of kids sitting in their rooms, playing on computers and watching DVDs one after the other, that will be another massive leap to help with children's health. That's really unhealthy in my view and you have to ask yourself what you would rather have, your kids sitting in their rooms or being out and doing what I used to get up to, playing the big time Bugsy Malone.

Like most young boys in any era, I got up to mischief and paid the price for it. There was the time when I took half a crown out of my mother's purse - stole would be the better word - and I thought I had got away with it. As I said we weren't exactly multi-millionaires so she realised what had happened pretty quickly. As I was the only one in the house when it happened, the evidence against me was certain. When she asked me about it I denied it of course, the act of desperation from a child, thinking of the smack which was going to come my way if I admitted my wrongdoing. That ringing sound in the ear as a well-aimed palm came thudding into the side of your head, tended to worry you a bit. She didn't accuse me but said, she was going upstairs and she expected to see the money on the television when she came down later. It was there of course and it taught me a lesson as I never did it to her ever again, even though I still got up to worse misdemeanours in the community on occasion. Unfortunately, I didn't learn too well from my previous experience. At school I decided to take an audio tape from the teacher's desk with some friends. The man wasn't too pleased when he discovered what had happened and called the police. They arrived and took us to the police station where we were grilled pretty hard by the officers. After a while, the others were allowed home and their parents picked them up, but mine didn't arrive and I was left on my own terrified.

Apparently, when they had called my mother, she said that she would pick me up in her own time. It sounds harsh, I know but she had decided to let me stew in my own juices for a while and it was probably the best thing.

When she did arrive, she headed straight for me and smacked me hard across the face. Kids don't realise the embarrassment they can heap on their parents sometimes. It provided the policemen with some amusement if nothing else. A few days later, we were called back and officially cautioned. I'll never forget Headlam Street Police Station in the Byker area of the city, even though it's long gone.

From the start, making money was a major factor in everyone's lives, any source would do. At the bottom of the estate was a pub called the Corner House and it had one of those built-on off licences that were around in the 60's. Around the back of the place they had built some sheds, where they kept the empty returned pop bottles. Three of my friends were called Pog, Philly and Brian and we knew every trick in the book for generating cash. They talk about recycling today but that was one of the first examples of it. You would get a deposit return on the bottles you brought back. I found a way into the sheds and used to watch the owner of the off licence carry his bottles to them and half an hour later I would go in, pick them up and return them. The money from that was always handy.

We had the system down to a T, swapping clothes or wearing glasses, anything to disguise ourselves from the bloke behind the off licence counter as we took the bottles back.

Another of my money making schemes involved the two paper rounds I had as a kid. As I filled my bag, I would take a few extra papers when the newsagent wasn't looking and sell them on the round. I didn't really regard that as something bad because the newsagent was a tight bloke and didn't pay that well.

Chocolate and bubblegum machines located on walls were another target and we developed a way of using a lolly stick with gum on the end as a way to take out the money. Telephone boxes were another source of income when we bunged up the slots, preventing the money dropping.

We had nowt and you have to remember that this was survival for us, without those scams we had nothing, and kids need some pleasure in their lives so the money from those things provided that. Children need to feel that they aren't disadvantaged and that was our way of coping.

When I was eleven years old, a film came out which had a massive effect on me. It was called Kes. The main character, a little lad, found and nurtured a kestrel and I was really touched by the idea of owning one of these magnificent hawks myself.

I knew Gosforth Park woods was a place I would find a kestrel's nest and eventually I found one with two young chicks and took one of them, pushing it down the front of my pullover and shinning back down the tree.

I know it was totally wrong now, but as a small boy you

don't think of those things. All I had in mind was bringing the bird up on my own and it being my personal property. Every day I would find suitable food for it, like slicing pieces off my mam's Sunday joint and I would chew it to a paste before feeding it, as well as searching for beetles and small animals.

I looked after that kestrel with a lot of love and attention, even building an amazing twig nest for it which took an age to do. A friend of mine got me a welder's glove so that I could hold the hawk, but on the first day I tried it, the bird had grown its flight feathers and it took off from my wrist and never came back.

There was a kestrel which regularly flew overhead in High Heaton and I couldn't help wondering if it was mine. I loved that bird so much.

Animals were an important part of my childhood, particularly an Alsatian dog that I called Jethro after the band Jethro Tull. A friend of mine asked me to look after him. I only had him for a week or two before the lad asked me for him back and that devastated me.

I never had enough money to buy an animal of my own so I used to go newt hunting in nearby Gosforth woods, keeping them in a jar at home until my brother told me it was cruel and released them back into a pond.

Animal relationships seemed destined to fail after these things happened, so I turned my attention to friends around the doors. Children's games played a big part of our lives then. My particular favourite was a game called knocky nine doors, where you would knock on a door, then try and get away before the owner came out.

It was a bit too tame for me in its original form. I wanted to see the confusion and anger on the owner's face as they came out time and again so I used to hide in bushes after tying a thread to the knocker in the twilight. Most of the time, they never spotted the thread and must have been frustrated as hell when it happened. A couple of times, I got caught and had a really hard clip around the ear but it never stopped me doing it. For some reason I nearly always picked on the local spinster who would storm out when her door went, screaming about knowing who it was and that she would sort them out.

Japs and English was another popular game. Half of us would play the Japanese army and half the English army, from the Second World War. We would carry pieces of wood as rifles and ambush each other, pretending to shoot one another. It was a great game and we would spend the whole day playing it, carrying our sandwiches and a bottle of water in our school haversack. When the water was shared around it would fill with bread floaters and the last man to drink had a meal instead of liquid but it never bothered us.

Cannon was a game played with an old tin can and a ball. You would place the can in the middle of the road and then each person would try and hit it. Whoever hit the can shouted a name and that person had to get the ball while the others ran from the scene. The name shouted was always the person who was disliked. They had to get the hard rubber ball and chase the group, trying to hit them with it. It wasn't pitched gently either. They would try and get you on the back right between the shoulder blades and it usually stung like mad. It made your eyes water too.

For most of my life, I have suffered with an ankle problem. As kids, my brothers were always off in the woods playing and I would have to go and find them. As I searched for them one day, running through the trees, I sprinted across a hole in the ground which they had dug as a trap. It was covered in sticks to hide the hole and as I ran across it, the whole thing collapsed. I thought I'd broken my ankle but it turned out only to be sprained.

Who would let their kids go to the woods alone today? With so many dodgy characters around, it's very unsafe. It's always been a problem and when I was young, a guy tried to pick me up while I was fishing in North Shields.

The incident sticks in my mind and thinking about the problems children have today, I feel its important to mention it. Unfortunately, children are too trusting and I was the same when I was very young.

I was nine years old and had gone fishing with a friend. In those days, parents were more inclined to let their children off the leash a bit. My dad worked on the railway so I got a free rail pass and I borrowed my brother's so that my friend could get on the train for nothing too. At one point in the day, I asked my mate to lend me his rod because he had a proper fishing pole and I only had a fishing line. He said no and I stomped off to the toilet in a really foul huff.

I don't need to go into details, but while I was there I was approached by a man with black teeth and national health glasses who was clearly interested in me sexually. He asked me if I was there on my own and if my parents were with me. When I told him they weren't, he suggested we go for a walk. Stupidly, I said I would but had to tell my mate first which he wasn't pleased about and he came with me.

My mate just said one word, hom, which is used in Newcastle for a homosexual. To this day I never realised just how lucky I'd been and God knows what would have happened if I hadn't gone to see my mate before going for a walk with the bloke.

I didn't know how dangerous it was then but at least I managed to get away from him. Having talked to friends about it, I discovered that a few of them had been approached by men like this and they were not as lucky as I was.

The point I'm making is that paedophilia isn't a modern thing. It's been around from the beginning of time. As a grandfather now, the whole thing sickens me and I worry about the fact that there seems to be more and more instances of it today. I know what I'd like to do to these degenerates. They wouldn't have the ability to perform their sickening practices, believe me. They should all be castrated.

To this day my dodgy ankle collapses on me at will. It's enough just to walk across a matchstick for it to go on me. Many years after I got the injury it happened in front of the Queen. I was in the winning enclosure at Ascot, in front of all those well-to-do racegoers and, for no reason, the thing decided it was time to have another relapse. I ended arse over tit and Her Majesty must have thought I had been drinking, but in reality I only had a drop.

Any money I made on the cash making schemes as a kid went to my brother George who was two years younger than me and didn't get to do much of the playing that the rest of us did.

He suffered really bad asthma attacks and was poorly all the time. Every couple of weeks, he would take a really bad turn for the worse, so I used to sit with him for hours just talking. For a little lad like me it was really scary to see his thin body getting worse and worse and hear the rasping breaths he used to take to get some air into his lungs.

In the end, he got so bad he was taken to hospital and spent two years there, only being allowed home for Christmas. The hospital was in Morpeth about twenty miles away and we could only visit him on a Saturday as we had no car.

What he really liked were those glow-in-the-dark figures of Frankenstein and Godzilla. I must have spent hours making them for him just to see a smile on his face. It was worth it for me to give him a bit of pleasure and to see him pull round for a couple of hours.

I once asked my mam if she had three wishes what would she want and she said she only wanted one and that was for George to get better.

After all the nursing and time I'd spent talking to him, I heard that he'd started smoking and I could have killed him. He eventually got better thank God but how everyone coped was a miracle and how he put up with everything I will never know.

CHAPTER THREE

TEENS AND THE TOON

For any kid moving up to senior school from the juniors, it's a frightening experience. Even before the first day, tales would be relayed about bullying and fighting and I was terrified of going into the unknown from the comfort of the juniors.

My brother Ronny was already in the senior school so I was luckier than most to have someone to advise and protect me a bit. I knew most of the hard lads who went there too so I made sure I avoided them that first year.

My mam had scraped around and got me a new uniform on tick so I was proud as punch when I made my way to school that first morning, dressed in new blazer, school tie, long pants and spanking new shoes. There was one big problem with those shoes - they had animal footprints on the sole and that wouldn't do my street cred any good, so I spent the morning trying to scrape off the embarrassing shapes. I knew if anyone saw them I would get a boatload of stick.

I used to walk to High Heaton Comprehensive every day.

It only took five minutes, but in that time I would pass the houses where my mates lived and by time we got to school there would be a gang of six of us, slagging off the teachers.

The school put me in class 1-6 for my first year but all my mates were in 1 South, which was the dunces' class, and all I wanted to do was be with them through school. I was proud of my positioning but like most kids I wanted to be in the cool class and that was 1 South. Crazy, I know, but that's how children's minds work.

Being born on the 24th August meant I was the youngest in the class and that didn't help either. If I had been born six days later, I would have been in the year below. On that first day, I met up with a mate of mine and he pointed out the local tom boy. He told me to call her a cow and I went up to her, saying it directly into her face. It was a big mistake because she punched me in the eye. I was panicking and trying to get away from her (at least I think it was a her) but she grabbed me and ripped the blazer off my back. When I went back to get it, she laced me again. By this time, my eye was totally shut, she looked at me and asked if I wanted some more. My head went down and I slunk away to find my mate who was laughing his head off. That was one learning experience I never forgot.

If I thought I was going to get any sympathy from my mam when I got home, I was wrong. She told me I deserved it and then went mad about the blazer, as if my male pride wasn't hurt enough. The girl was a tough nut and I found out later that she played hockey for the school team and even played rugby. I didn't bother her again.

Starting senior school seemed to coincide with me getting into regular trouble. I absolutely hated assembly and did everything in my power to miss it or at least made sure I was regularly late for it, The teachers gave up trying to make me attend after a few times of this behaviour.

I wasn't the only one to avoid it, the others and I used to tell them that we were in the R.E. room, talking about family problems.

The R.E. teacher had given us a key to let ourselves in when we told him about the family discussions. Actually, what we did was play three card brag and smoke. When the Headmaster found out what we were doing, he sacked the poor bloke and used his favourite answer on us for stepping out of line, the cane. Six of the best with a cane is no picnic and how a grown man could do that to a boy was beyond me. He seemed to take some sadistic pleasure in it.

Even today I can remember the first time he bent me over. The pain was horrendous and I went home to inspect the damage in my mam's dressing table mirror. Big red welts covered the flesh and looked angry.

This bloke had a floor in his study covered in black and white tiles and he had marked out one with red electrician's tape because he knew he could get his best swipe in if you were standing on that tile. How sick is that?

He wanted to cane me once when I had received his punishment the day before and I told him he couldn't do it because my backside was red raw. He just grabbed me by the neck, bent me over the desk and thrashed me over the legs. You didn't get away from him when he wanted his fun. When others got the slipper, I used to laugh at them. It was nowhere near as painful as the cane and, over time, my backside got used to it. When he delivered his final blow, I would grin at him, he hated me for that.

I sat outside the Head's study so much that I looked like a permanent fixture and one teacher would always see me there and ask me why I was waiting. I would tell him it was for smoking, fighting or whatever and he would shake his head and walk away. Once he questioned me about it and I said that I had been caught with a gun. The expression on his face was amazing. He told me that I was going to end up like Al Capone and wandered off in astonishment. I didn't tell him that it was a spud gun, it kept my mystique intact.

Even if I played the wag, I still managed to get to the dinner hall at lunch time. I know most kids hate school dinners but I loved them. The food was fantastic in those days and we probably appreciated it more because the family had nothing. With six kids in our family, we were entitled to free school meals, getting a ticket which had to be put into a box when you arrived in the dining room. When I put my ticket into the box, I used to take two out and go back. Seconds and thirds were never refused. My mates, Maddo, Smithy, Philly and Johnny Rouse, loved the food too and we would all do the necessary to get more. Poor old Johnny got cancer I heard and died in his twenties. It's such a shame because I loved that lad at school.

I haven't always been the sharpest tool in the box. When our Ronny left to start work, I used to wear his best clothes for school until the day he caught me when I was pictured on a class photograph in his best jacket. He gave me a thick ear for that.

One teacher actually assaulted me physically. Someone had made a comment in the class and I got the blame for it. He took me outside and punched and kicked me all over the place. If I had done what he accused me of, I probably would have accepted it but this was totally unfair.

When I told my mam, she was up as fast as a bullet from a gun and of course he denied it, but it did happen. The bastard even ripped Ronny's shirt and jacket which I was wearing but my mother saw Ronny all right about that, even though he wanted to kill me.

Later on at school I became known as the Judge. I decided for some reason that we would set up a court for the kids who stepped out of line. It was all done tastefully with two guards marching the accused in front of me to answer the charges.

Usually all they were guilty of was wearing daft clothes or grassing on someone but that was a minor point. The accused would make pleas as to why they were innocent and I would sit there and listen in my capacity as decider of the facts.

Actually, it didn't matter what they said because I always found them guilty - so much for justice. At that point I would don the black cap which we kept for the event and dispense my sentence, which usually meant a few well-aimed blows on the arms just to teach them a lesson. In most cases they didn't deserve it.

It backfired on me a couple of times when the lads grabbed me and did the same to me. The first time it was for wearing my hippy brother's jacket and after the second I scrapped the court altogether.

I was never much of a scholar but I did like French, I loved swimming and was in the swimming team. Everyday I used to go to the local pool and practice before I went to school. A few lengths set me up for the day but the problem was I hated the teacher in charge of the team and I left after a while. That was a major disappointment. I don't think I would have made a Duncan Goodhew but I was very passable in the water then. Although my ankle still gave me a lot of pain, swimming was about the only sport I could cope with.

One of the strange things about my schooldays was my hatred of music. Maybe it was the teacher with what I called the concerto haircut, a parting down the middle and flicked up over the ears. Perhaps that's why he was an obnoxious little shit. His attitude stunk where the kids were concerned and I don't think he was liked by one of them. These days I love music, am self taught on the guitar and listen to my favourites all the time, but that bloke could have destroyed my love for music very early in my life.

Looking back on it now, I must have been a really tough little bugger to teach but it's interesting to see that I am now on their website as a former pupil, such is a bit of fame.

When I reached fifteen, I was going through the transition from boy to man like most of my mates. Since that time, I have always been a very virile bloke but those first feelings of sexual awakenings were really strong for me. At one point, I had been causing some trouble at school and was ordered to spend a week in the Headmaster's office. It was no bad thing because the secretary was a really attractive woman with auburn hair and she wore the shortest skirts imaginable.

The desk they gave me was right opposite hers and I could see her stocking tops and underwear all the time. I'm positive she made sure that I could see purposely by the way she sat. It was totally unfair to a young lad going through the feelings of manhood and I would disappear to the Head's toilet regularly to get some relief.

At least those feelings of virility are diminishing now I'm

getting older and I'm quite pleased about it. Sometimes I would feel ill at the intensity of them and I'm sure I was no different to 95% of all young lads going through this. I wanted to put this story in because I know a lot of young men have those feelings and feel that they can't discuss it with anyone.

On the day I was due to leave school, I approached the Headmaster and asked if I could stay on. He just laughed and laughed and I realised that all the bother I had caused had come home to roost. It was time to move on into the real world and I was terrified.

We did some great things as youngsters. Apple and pear raiding was a regular pastime. Owners would go to bed at night to trees full of juicy fruit, only to wake up next morning to stripped branches and no evidence of where it had all gone. Occasionally we were caught and got a clipped ear for the trouble but it was worth it.

As a young lad in the 1970s I had a wonderful time. I don't think we'll ever see an era like that again. Everything just seemed to be right, from the clothes to the music. The 60s were over and music seemed to be moving into a new level of experimentation and its diversity was amazing. The charts reflected that variety of music too. You would get Slade alongside Jethro Tull and the Osmonds, but it didn't seem to matter. Lifetime musical tastes were formed then and I am pleased to see that young people today still want 70s party tracks for dancing and listening to.

Newcastle was a city of change then. It was beginning the transition to the pristine place it is today but back then there were huge areas of pre-war housing being demolished to make way for new estates. The building sites were a playground for kids and a lot of them were hurt scrabbling around in the rubble, but the new dwellings had indoor toilets which were a luxury for most people. There was a lot of money to be made by people, salvaging from the sites.

It was quite strange in my house, I had five brothers who were all hairies and there was me, the lone skinhead in my crombie, white T-shirt, braces, short jeans and bovver boots. When I think back, I must have been the only skinhead in the world listening to Black Sabbath and Jethro Tull.

Skinheads were getting a lot of bad publicity at the time and my hippy brothers would give me a hiding regularly just for being one of the clan. At least I kept the neighbourhood guessing in those days because they would never see me out in the same colour boots twice. What they didn't know was that it was always the same pair of Doc Martins I wore but I would regularly paint them a different colour, one day blue, the next day yellow and so on. Who says I couldn't be a fashion designer too?

In those days it was fashionable to be in a gang and I was a member of the HAB or Heaton Aggro Boys. We proudly carried the badge on our blue Harrington jackets but really there was little aggro undertaken. We even had a song that someone had come up with. The words were simple but apt;

Big brown boots and yellow laces
Turned up trousers and fancy braces
We are the lads that will smash your faces
We are the Heaton Aggro.

I was stopped one day by two policemen who asked me what HAB stood for and I told them it meant handsome and beautiful which didn't go down well. One of them wasn't impressed and told me I was a smart arse before hitting me across the nose with his torch. My nose was wrecked, not broken, but it collapsed the nasal passageways. The interesting thing is I wasn't doing anything wrong.

As a skinhead you were a member of your own area and heaven help you if you bumped into a gang from a rival locality. One of my mates from that time got a hell of a beating just walking down a road and coming across a rival set of lads. It was really bad.

It was worse again if you were a hairy and came across some skinheads. I remember my brother going to the fish shop and being set on because of his hair.

My mother asked me to go and when I got to the fish shop one of the skinheads proudly held me in the air in my Harrington and boots, calling me little skinhead. It was the same lad who had nearly killed my brother but that's the way it was back then, mad but true.

There wasn't even much fighting, despite what the papers said in those days. The sheer numbers in the gangs was enough to scare rival gangs away but that's the press for you, if there isn't a story, they'll make one up.

It was tough back then but the best thing about it was, there wasn't the level of drug culture that there is today. We got our buzz in those days from the odd bottle of cider or a big can of Party 7, not sticking our heads in a bag full of glue.

The women were so beautiful then as well, in their ultra-short minis, platform shoes, embroidered sheepskin coats and curly perms. The sheepskins were similar to the afghans of the time but not so long or smelly.

One of the local churches, St. Georges, had a disco which was the only place to meet girls and have a dance but it was cancelled after a bit of trouble one night so we turned to the

Newton Park pub which had a disco on Friday nights. Most of the people were much older than me, I was fifteen at the time, but I always managed to blag my way in one way or another. My older brothers' birth certificate came in useful during those attempts and when my mates got nicked I would lift a pint in their direction and smile as they were ejected.

For a time, when Newcastle wasn't the party city it is now, there was a lot of glitter around in the nightclubs giving them a sort of fairy tale quality among the depressing housing, which identified the place as a typical downbeat northern city.

The Oxford Galleries in the 70s was a forward thinking enterprise and used to put on special under-sixteen discos on Saturday mornings with dancing and soft drinks for the young people attending. It was my first experience of an adult entertainment venue, where we could meet girls and have a good time. Unfortunately for me, my first visit was a bit of a disaster. I was dancing with a girl, when a ring of youths formed around us. It was really frightening and I didn't know what was going on until one lad moved in and smashed me in the face. His mate was next and he kicked the hell out of me.

It's a wonder that I ever went back to a nightclub after that. Places like the Mayfair, Tiffany's, Cavendish and the Dolce Vita will be familiar to anyone from the North East who read this book. They were the haunts of nearly everyone from Thursday night through to Saturday in those days and they served us well by taking our mind off some of the working days to follow.

Quality restaurants were a novelty in Newcastle, people just didn't eat out much then. It was a real treat and chefs weren't as common as they are today. Fanny Craddock and the galloping gourmet were the limit of T.V. chefs in the 70s. Fanny's food was good and wholesome but lacked some of the exotic feel you see today and the Galloping Gourmet offerings were always rich and full of butter and cream. In many ways I wish those glorious days would come back.

CHAPTER FOUR

WORK, WORK, WORK

I got into cooking at school. It was at a time when attitudes were changing in education and practical subjects such as metalwork, woodwork, domestic science and needlework became available to all.

The cookery teacher had particularly nice legs so it wasn't much of a surprise that a lot of boys chose to attend her lessons. The sap was rising in the growing lads and I can remember the first lesson well; we fired questions at her about her love life but she kept changing the subject back to cooking. Throughout that first meeting her face was beetroot red. It wasn't the best educational reason to choose a class but young lads don't think in those terms.

Our first attempted recipe was rock cakes. The ones that I produced could have been used by the army as a new type of weapon, they were certainly hard enough to break windows as I amply demonstrated. Our teacher warned us to be careful about the amount of sugar we used, saying they would be too hard if we used too much. The lad next to me went to the toilet and I took the opportunity to empty a whole bag of sugar into his mix. Strangely enough, I got into trouble about that but it mustn't have done too much to put me off as I stayed in the class, learning the basics of cooking.

Once a week, we attended the local college to improve our knowledge, although to be fair, we paid more attention to the girls than the food. It was the Polytechnic in the Haymarket area of Newcastle and the women there were outstanding.

At lunch we would all disappear to the local pub for a few pints so when we got back the lecturers knew the afternoon would be a washout as far as teaching went.

Although I enjoyed cooking, my first real job on leaving school was working in a garage. Girls were interesting me and I needed the money to take them out. Up to this point I had been very shy around the opposite sex but I was gradually conquering my fears. Let's be honest, I was rapidly conquering my fears.

Living with five brothers and a dad who were real men, my exposure to women was limited to my mother and some of her friends before this time and now the sheer animal passion I was feeling was beginning to dominate my life.

All young men go through this period in their lives and, like everybody else, I found it difficult to cope with and a very frustrating time.

There were relationships I drifted in and out of with skinhead girls at the time. Some of the lasses were rough, and I really mean rough, and the final straw came when I started going out with a girl who had a tattoo on her forehead, even I thought it was time to move on to a better class of woman.

Two days before I left school, I ran to Benton Road where

some garages were situated. One of them was a company called Minories which was a big motor company in Newcastle at the time. Shaking with nerves I asked to see the foreman of the workshop, asking him if they had any jobs as apprentice mechanics. There were none but he offered me a position as an apprentice paint sprayer at £11 a week so I took it.

They sent me to college again for one day a week to learn the trade. Frankly, the lecturer was a bit of a bastard. He had taught my brother on an earlier occasion. For some reason my brother must have upset this man because at roll call on the first morning when he came across the name Miller, he asked if I had a brother called Richard. I was bursting for the toilet when I replied yes and asked if I could go. His sarcastic reply was, 'Yes but remember, anymore than three shakes is masturbating'. It was done so sarcastically and just to embarrass me in front of the course members. The laughter from the lads on the rest of the course really cut into me.

From that moment he looked for any excuse to report me to the head of the college and I knew that my number was up there.

On the day I started at Minories, six other apprentices were lined up with me, ready to learn the trade. The usual initiations began, I was asked to go for a tin of tartan paint, then a left-handed screwdriver and finally a long stand. Not much work was done that first day and I really enjoyed myself.

The old Commer vans and wagons were the first vehicles I worked on, along with the occasional car when I was lucky. Gritter wagons with tapered hoppers for distributing the road salt were the only things the lads would let me spray because no one saw the inside of them. As I climbed out of the first one, proud of my first real painting job, Tony and Stew, my workmates, collapsed laughing. I had forgotten to wear the special hat for the job and my hair and face were bright yellow, I looked like a canary and it creased them up.

One thing stuck in my mind about the older lads who worked in the spray booths, every one of them suffered chronic chest problems. As they walked and talked, the heavy raspy breathing from them was terrible and I knew that the spray painting trade wasn't for me.

There was always a bit of carry on at the garage. For the first year all you can do is rub cars down and the emery takes the skin off your finger ends in no uncertain fashion and that causes pain.

It was one of the first cars I had worked on, when I told one of the lads that my fingers were really painful. He pointed to a bucket with some liquid in it and told me to dip my hands in and that would soothe it. I followed his advice. Seconds after I plunged them in, there was the most excruciating burning sensation and I was hopping around the paint bays, screaming in agony.

Everyone was laughing and I discovered that the liquid was paint stripper. Those are the type of little in jokes you have to put up with in the motor trade. I've never panicked so much in my whole life but everyone I ran to get help from just smiled and kept silent when I was pleading with them. Eventually, I hit the toilets and plunged my hands in cold water, not knowing that was the best neutraliser. God was on my side again. Water takes away the effects of paint stripper quickly so I wasn't in pain too long. If the Health and Safety Executive had been in existence when I was working in that garage, they'd have been shut down in an instant because of some of the horseplay that went on.

There was the time I went to work and everyone was being nice to me until the lads lured me to the storeroom, grabbed me and removed my trousers, daubing my town halls in underseal. They were laughing at me telling me they would never rust, it wasn't funny for me at all.

Two days later they did it again, only this time they used grease. It had taken me two days of rubbing with all sorts of thinners etc to get the underseal off so I knew I was in for a long period of cleaning. Tears were rolling down my face at the pain of the burning liquid.

I've mentioned that I had to attend college as part of my apprenticeship and it was around this time that I called the tutor an arsehole as a result of his attitude towards me and the college expelled me.

My job was reliant on me going for the lessons there so my boss at work called me in and sacked me. I pleaded with him, breaking down because I desperately needed the job but he wouldn't listen to anything I said. You've no idea how much I wanted to tell him how much bullying I'd taken in his precious business but I kept my mouth shut.

From that moment on, work was a dirty word for me and I hated the thought of being in any employment. It was so bad that I wished I was back at school.

Some of my other jobs haven't exactly been the bee's knees. I moved to a plumbers' merchants where I used to remove the toilets from the lorries coming into the company. It was a boring job, believe me.

While I was at the plumbers' merchants something happened which, looking back, I am not proud of. I began to take things from the cash and carry company next door. We offloaded their wagons as well as our own and on one occasion, I took a box of chocolates while removing stock.

I was asked to attend a meeting with the boss the following morning and he asked me how long I had been stealing. When I told him that was the first time, he sacked me on the spot. If the truth be known, I had been doing it for a while and now it's something I am not proud of at all. I was lucky they didn't call the police.

At this point I was sick of my life, I had no job and had been causing my mother sleepless nights with my attitude and the fact that I had brought the police to her door with the tape recorder incident. I desperately needed something positive to happen and to turn my life around. If my boss had been vindictive, he could easily have called the police and I would have had a criminal record which, to this day, I have never had, thanks to the fact that he gave me a chance. That was the turning point for me.

I've mentioned the Tarmac briefly and that was my next job; like most things in life, getting that job came as a bit of luck. I was in the local working men's club and an old man was in there who I knew worked on the roads. When I asked him if he thought there were any jobs going, he told me that his boss was coming in that day and he would speak to him for me.

When the man did arrive, the old road layer told me to introduce myself. I was a bit nervous, bearing in mind how I had lost my previous job but I just went up and spoke to him. The interview consisted of him asking me if I could dig and when I told him that I dug my mam and dad's garden every week, it seemed enough for him and he hired me on the spot.

No high-powered interview technique in those days.

At seventeen you are naturally nervous anyway and when the van turned up for me on Monday morning I was terrified.

As I climbed in, I was amazed at the characters. First was Dougy, who looked more like a gypsy with his black hair turning grey, long sideburns, Mexican tash, massive earrings and sovereign rings on each finger, which could have seriously reduced Britain's gold reserve if they had gone missing. Charlie was a quiet, hippy type who just sat there smiling all the time. He was an ex gravedigger and you could see how it would appeal to him.

Old Joe was sixty-four years old and he loved to talk. Brian, the gaffer, was a slim man with the biggest double chin I've ever seen. It seems beer was the morning tipple as he was taking it down in massive gulps. He asked me if I had any money with me and I told him a tenner. It was the worst thing I could have said, from that moment I became his drink feeder. Brian was always pleading poverty so it was left to me to buy his ale. I reckon if he had stopped drinking, Scottish & Newcastle Breweries' shares would have plummeted.

The Tarmac gangs like this really bonded together. You could be dying but still get out for work in the morning so that you wouldn't let your mates down. I've seen blokes who shouldn't have been out of bed, struggling to work and putting in a full day of hard physical graft just to make sure their mates would be paid for getting the job done. These ponces today who stay off because they have a headache just make my blood boil.

These lads were ruthless and anything that wasn't tied down was taken. Most of the stuff they took was from sites we worked on, fencing, kerbs or anything else which they could use in their gardens.

When we worked on a night shift in Sunderland, one of the lads had noticed a rack of shirts close to the letterbox of a shop. Going to the van, he sawed the prongs off one of the Tarmac rakes, leaving just two in place.

Back at the shop, he slipped his new tool through the letterbox and lifted the shirts one by one, off the rack and back through the door. Our gang was the smartest squad on the block that night.

One job in Newcastle had us working in the Grainger Market during the night and the stalls for the market still had their goods on display. The boys raided the lot.

It seemed that everyone wanted Tarmac jobs done throughout the 70s and 80s so we travelled throughout the North East and North West plying the trade. It wasn't always sweetness and light though. Dougy didn't like me at all and he was a real hard individual from Walker in Newcastle. Someone to avoid like the plague, but I just couldn't get away from him picking on me and bullying me. It wasn't unusual for him to punch me in the face just for the hell of it.

I think Charlie really regretted leaving his job as a gravedigger. He certainly didn't like the Tarmac as much as doing that and he seemed to have had a real pride in preparing the sacred ground for the dead. It wouldn't have surprised me to see him popping up in a film like Night of the Living Dead.

In the North East, we have an excellent reputation for growing and old Joe was an expert at producing vegetables. I asked him once how he grew such massive leeks and onions. His secret lay at the butcher's. The butcher would regularly provide him with animal blood which he spread on the soil and Joe swore by the results of this treatment.

One morning he brought me in a brown ale ice lollipop. Can you imagine a worse concoction, but he was so proud of it. I told him it was lovely when in reality it was one of the most bloody awful things I've ever tasted. I just didn't want to hurt the man's feelings but I'll never forget pushing it down. It still gives me shivers. Outdoor jobs like the Tarmac are reliant on the weather, so we constantly prayed for rain. If we got that, we got a day off at full pay. You can imagine we looked for any sign of precipitation.

There was one 10 ton laying job which we had managed to lay in light rain amazingly and as soon as the blackstuff was down the waterworks turned off.

None of us were too keen to do anymore for the day so Brian suggested we roll around in puddles and say we had been soaked to the skin. Can you imagine passing motorists seeing five grown men reeling around in roadside water and the comments? Charlie was standing next to the road when a bus tore through a massive puddle, soaking him from head to foot. He was laughing at us because he knew he was the most likely to be given the day off.

It worked. the boss accepted we should have the rest of the day off and so we went to the nearest pub just to make us as wet on the inside as we were on the outside.

As I've said, a Tarmac gang is a bonded group so when the company wanted to split us up, none of us were pleased. Brian visited me and he was absolutely fuming at the decision. He wanted us all to refuse to go to any other gang and in some ways I agreed with him. The problem was that the heavy drinking in the gang was catching up with me.

There were days when we had left the job and started

drinking and I would find myself lying in my bed the next morning, still dressed in my working clothes which were smelly from the job. My mother blasted me every morning and threatened me that she would go out to the van to have it out with my mates about the states I was coming home in.

Eventually, I decided it would be better if I went to another gang. Lar Groves was the gaffer of the new group they put me in. The problem was that he enjoyed the drink almost as much as Brian. That was where the similarity ended though. Lar was a real baby and he would go into huff after huff. I was glad to see the back of him.

Billy Callas was my next road gang boss. I really thought the world of him. He was an ex army man and had boxed for his regiment. Billy was probably the nicest bloke I've ever met, he looked after his lads and got the respect he deserved in return. I saw the rest of my time out on the Tarmac in his gang and loved every minute of it. I think Billy might have had a bit of a fondness for me because he always paid a bit more attention and gave me advice and help whenever I needed it. Those are things you appreciate when you are a young lad starting out on your working life.

His right hand man was called Eddy and he was a really nice man too. It was so funny because he used to lecture his daughters on not getting pregnant, which is a very responsible thing to do. The only problem was that they were six, eight and ten years of age. He was so serious about it and we all had a bit of a laugh behind his back.

One day, he arrived at work to tell us that he had made a pass at his wife's best friend while walking home and his wife had left him after her friend told her about the incident. Maybe he should have lectured himself. The poor bloke was forty eight years old and had to start again.

The nature of the road laying business is that, sometimes you are mixed up between gangs when it's necessary. It breaks up the monotony a bit. There was a time when I joined a gang run by a man called Jacky and I have to say that his gang were a bunch of lunatics.

Jacky himself had been in Durham prison and he looked evil. I never had the guts to ask him why he had been in jail and I don't think it would have gone down too well if I had. He was fixated about his wife's father dying of cancer and had been with him when he died. It was all he could ever talk about; for a young lad it wasn't the best conversation in the world.

The closeness of the men in road gangs is outstanding, it reminds me of the camaraderie in the kitchen. They were men's men on the Tarmac and I had some great times working away. As the youngest member of these gangs, I had the mickey taken out of me all the time but I loved it. Practical jokes happened in the road laying business too.

On numerous occasions, the lads grabbed me and inserted a brush through the back of my sleeves. I couldn't move and spent the rest of the day wandering around like Worzel Gummidge. Sometimes they would even tie me up against a lamp-post at the side of the road and pull my trousers and underpants down. It was one of the most embarrassing things which has ever happened to me as the toots and whistles started from the passing motorists.

One day, a couple of the lads positioned the chocolate box or portaloo facing the motorway. I went in to deal with business, not knowing they had fixed the lock and tied string to the handle. One tug on the string and I was exposed to the passing traffic, including a bus with astonished passengers seeing this hideous sight. The box was made of tin and a well aimed brick tossed by one of the lads was enough to make you finish your business in record time.

Tarmac lads don't tend to be Tom Cruise lookalikes, they are usually basic men as described here but I was always amazed at the amount of women living in areas near the work, who would offer themselves to us. Some of them were not exactly Catherine Zeta-Jones lookalikes but it was the respectable middle-class ones that were the surprise. Sex in the afternoon was a regular occurrence. Come to think of it, sex at anytime was a typical event.

There were many times when the women would see us working in the cold and bring us a hot cup of tea on the job. There would always be a fight about whose turn it was to take the cups back. On one estate in North Shields the lads did more shagging than work.

Even my mother wasn't untouchable to the Tarmac lads. One morning she was walking along the road as the van came along. She wasn't familiar with our transport then and I told the boys to sound the horn and whistle at her while I kept my head down. It was funny to watch her preening herself as she thought there were some blokes interested.

When I got home and told her how it had all come about, she clouted me hard. It didn't matter how old you were to my mam, retribution was swift and painful.

A few weeks later, she was late for work when the boys arrived to pick me up on a Monday morning. They offered her a lift and she climbed in the back of the dirty van, among the empty beer cans and the work tools.

By the time she got out at the place where she worked, she

was feeling quite sick. A Tarmac laying van with five people inside after a weekend's drinking and curry eating was a place of many and varied odours. It wasn't for the faint hearted, the unpleasant bodily fumes persuaded her never to accept a lift from us ever again.

CHAPTER FIVE

COULDN'T BOX EGGS

Any sort of training was out for me having sprained my ankle as a child. At school PE was a nightmare because I didn't want to do it and would do anything to get out of it.

The trouble was, I wanted to enter the sports days and win a prize. It was a bit of a juggling act trying to get out of PE lessons and still enter the competitions. Somehow I managed it and I remember entering the cross country one year, coming a miserable last.

I did swim for the school and was quite successful at that, but any sort of planned lesson activity wasn't for me.

At fifteen I came across some weights in the gym. It was one of those life-changing happenings and the feeling of a new purpose overwhelmed me. I began lifting the weights and was enjoying myself greatly when the PE teacher came in. The moment he saw me he told me to put them down and get out of his gym. I had that kind of effect on the whole teaching staff for some reason.

I started weight training in earnest from that moment and it took over my life completely. Never having wanted to be involved in PE at school, the moment I left the place, I joined a gym. Everyday I ate, slept and drank weights. It was all I ever wanted to do.

The gym I joined was at Killingworth in North Tyneside and a lot of the people there got involved with steroid taking but I was never one for that, avoiding it like the plague. Maybe I was a bit of a chicken because a lot of the blokes had better physiques than mine but it didn't matter to me, drugs have never been my bag.

I'm proud of the fact that I once managed three hundred press ups in ten minutes, for me it was always about fitness, not illegal substances.

I got a bit bored with lifting weights after a while and joined Shipley Street boxing club where I could continue weight training and use it a bit more practically. The club still exists today and is going strong. I always enjoyed the fitness aspect of the club and the hard training we used to do. It was something that really appealed to me.

The first time I ever boxed was as a child at Christmas. Every year my dad would buy a pair of boxing gloves for all his sons, despite the fact that my mam always went mad with him for doing it. She always told him that no more boxing gloves were coming into the house and, lo and behold, the next festive season we had some more. My brothers and I would spar and box all the time and sometimes it would get a bit strong, it wasn't unusual for one of us to get hurt or bloodied but we thoroughly enjoyed it.

The North East has a fine tradition of boxing heroes who have done well over the years; Paul Lister fought for the

British title; Glen McCrory was World Champion, John Westgarth fought for the European title and he was really unlucky. If he had won that fight he would have fought Michael Spinks. We also had John Davidson and Billy Hardy, who is my step daughter Julie's partner.

I used to train with John Westgarth and Paul Lister often and mainly when they had a fight coming off. We did general road and fitness training together and I used to go along to keep them company through the lonely hours of hard work.

Sometimes, when I had taken leave of my senses, I would put on the gloves and get into the ring with them. One punch to the head used to finish me off but I never learned my lesson. They were friends of mine and never took liberties with me but if you are ever in the ring with a heavyweight boxer and he catches you with a punch, it's like a hammer blow has connected with your head.

Just before Glen McCrory won his world title bout, I had been living and training with John and on the night of his fight against Glen, John asked me to lead him into the ring. I was as proud as punch at that.

Leaving the dressing room, John placed his hands on my shoulders and we headed for the main boxing area. We were all on a massive high as we headed towards the ring.

It's just a pity that I took him the wrong way in front of 2000 people and the T.V. cameras at Gateshead Leisure Centre. I took him down the aisle which led to the toilets and I could hear the trainers screaming, "This way you fucking idiot", I felt so embarrassed.

John won the fight thank God but I never have got over the embarrassment of that incident. Looking back on that night, I always think Glen should have refused that fight, he was only a kid at the time and John was a mature twenty-eight-year-old with a lot of boxing experience behind him.

Of course Glen eventually had his day eventually when he won the World Cruiserweight title.

Maybe all this fired me up a bit because I went back to my boxing club and the trainer asked me to have a proper fight. I was twenty-four and too old to start boxing but I accepted. My attitude was, what the hell it's only one bout and what harm could that do. I'd helped the kids and I really wanted to show that I could do it. If I won a trophy, great, but the respect of the kids was the motivating part.

On the night of my fight three hundred people turned out to watch me but the lad I was supposed to box didn't turn up. The fight venue and date were changed to Workington the following week, where I would be fighting this bloke on his own turf.

At three o'clock on the day of the fight, I was picked up and we headed for Workington. When we got there I looked for the time of my fight and it wasn't scheduled until 10pm. My brother and a couple of friends who had gone down for the bout, sat around drinking but I just had to wait patiently until it was my turn to get into the ring. The longer it went on the more tense I became.

I'm a fairly big bloke and I weighed in at 12 stone 4 pounds and my opponent, who was small and stocky tipped the scales at 14 stone. I was already conceding quite a bit in weight.

Even today, years after the bout, I can still remember it as clear as day. I was so psyched up all I could see was the opponent and everything else around was a white out. In my mind I felt I was fighting for my life and when the bell rang for the first round I weighed in with everything I had.

He caught me a couple of times in the initial round and I staggered back to the stool, happy for a bit of rest. The trainer hit me in the face with the sponge which was a complete shock but I needed it to bring me round a bit. I was puffing and panting, the prospect of more rounds ahead wasn't the most pleasant thought I've ever had.

When I glanced into the other boxer's corner, my opponent was sitting with his arms folded and totally unconcerned. It was that moment when I knew boxing wasn't for me.

When the bell rang for the second round I absolutely shit myself with fear. He tore over and battered me all over the place. I winced at the sheer ferocity of the blows and eventually I sank to one knee and that was it. It was all over and not a second too soon for me.

When I got to my corner, I felt so depressed having let everyone down and the loser's trophy was reward for the effort but didn't make me feel any better. For years I wondered what had happened to my opponent and just by chance I was talking to a policeman one day at the gym I go to. He told me he was from Workington and I asked him about the lad I had fought. The policeman told me that he knew him and the lad was the hardest man in the town. He ran all the doors in the pubs and clubs, so it's probably best I went down in the second.

CHAPTER SIX

MEN IN BLACK

Nightlife in Newcastle during the 70s wasn't the sophisticated experience that it is today, there were a lot of seedy pubs and clubs in an area about a mile square, and like today, the city was heaving with revellers. We've always liked a drink and enjoying ourselves in this part of the world. The Quayside which is so frequented now was just a collection of corrugated iron sheds and industrial companies then. It's hard to believe that when you see the refined area it is now.

One of my favourite haunts at that time was Manhattan's, which was part of the Tuxedo Junction nightclub. I remember the tables had telephones on them and a directory with the numbers for other tables so if you saw a woman who took your fancy, you could call her table and talk to her before making a fool of yourself. Tuxedo's was just one of a number of clubs I visited at that time which included familiar names like Scamps, the Dolce Vita and Bentleys, and most of my weekends were spent in these exotic places.

This is the point in my life when I got a job working on the doors of the Newcastle clubs. It was an interesting experience to say the least because the mildest mannered, small blokes can transform into Mike Tyson with a couple of pints inside them. It's unfortunate for them, alcohol makes believe think they can take on the world.

Getting paid for something which was a laugh a minute was a bonus. It was like having a normal night on the town, full of drink and women and I took full advantage of it.

The Bigg Market was the place to be seen when I worked on the doors and it still is THE place today in Newcastle, along with the Quayside. I may be biased, but the women in the city are as beautiful as any I have seen anywhere. They take a great deal of time to make sure they look fantastic and some of the scanty clothing they wear has to be seen to be believed.

One evening I was having a night out in the city centre and was approached by Alan Scott who was the head doorman of the entire Bigg Market area. He asked me and a friend of mine, Paul, to join his team and gave us one of his main clubs to look after; it was called Pumphreys and was run by a gay couple.

This was my first real exposure to the gay community and the moment Paul and I came in their eyes bulged, you could tell from a mile away they fancied us and they started chatting us up from minute one. We politely told them to fuck off and that was the last problem they gave us.

A doorman's job is to look for trouble before the problem enters the premises. If a dodgy-looking mob turns up, it's your job to look for some reason to knock them back. It could be trainers or tattoos but I was always at a bit of a disadvantage with body art because I had them myself. Blokes used to say, "You're fucking kidding mate aren't you?" but as I told them, I was OUTSIDE the door.

Mobs are a bit of a problem. When they realise you're looking for a number of them in a big party, they just come in ones and two's instead and you don't realise they are together until the alarm sounds. Then it's all hands to the pump, rushing inside and facing twenty or thirty blokes kicking off.

Any bouncer will tell you when that happens to try and contain the trouble rather than aggravate it, so we would try to isolate them as quickly as possible. If the fighting was inevitable or had already started, we just waded in, fists blazing. Paul would drop anyone with just one dig but I had to fight for my life to get them out, all this for the princely sum of £12 a night. Fifty quid for four nights wasn't to be sniffed at but I really worked for my money. It had its compensations though when we got our drinks free and could get into any Newcastle night club for nowt.

It's a dangerous business working the doors of a nightclub, one night the buzzer went off and there we were running into the unknown. The fight was between two mobs and I'll never know how that many slipped through. It was a set up to get us because the moment we arrived other lads were waiting for us. I managed to grab one bloke and was glassed in the face by another. In a situation like that you don't have time to realise what's happened, you're fighting for your life and self preservation is the only thing on your mind.

Paul's first shot at anyone was in the midriff to double them over but this time there wasn't time for niceties, he was just laying them out cold one by one. I finally got to my feet and asked Paul to look at my face, he told me I would live and pitched me back into the fray.

I came away with a few stitches from that one and I felt very lucky. It was amazing the two of us could control the situation and to this day, I'll never know how we did it. We found out afterwards they were a well-known, hard mob from a place called West Denton and the following week they arrived back, this time double handed.

As we stood on either side of the door to the club, one of them came over and asked to see us so we crossed the road to talk to him. How stupid was that? When we got there and saw there were thirty or so of them we got a bit worried.

A big chunky lad, who was probably the leader, told us they had massive respect for us and shook our hands. They also said if we had bother in the future they would help us out. We went away from that encounter breathing out heavily.

In fairness, the bouncers I came across did their best to deal with any situation in as mild a manner as possible but some people just can't stop causing trouble and have to be stopped.

Paul was an interesting case, he was a heavyweight boxer who had fought Horace Notice for the British title so I felt safe in his company. Notice was in the same camp as Frank Bruno and Paul was doing well against him until Bruno got out of his seat to tell Notice to get serious. It was curtains for Paul from that point but he certainly gave Notice a run for his money.

When you're working with someone who looks like Paul and is as big as he is, the problem was trouble would always come my way and not his. Jim Robertson was the name of the man who employed me on the doors. He looked like one of the Bee Gees in his leather trousers.

Some of the men I worked with on the doors years ago are still there. They're nearly fifty now and I think they should be sitting on the settee at home rather than throwing drunks out of licensed premises, but it's their life and only they know why they are still doing it. Whatever it is, I feel that it can't be a good life. The older you get, the more chance there is of serious injury in that game. I was lucky, the only incidents which caused me a problem were a couple of glasses hitting me in the face and the odd punch thrown here and there.

You can get a bad reputation working on the doors but thankfully I never did. I always just wanted to be one of the lads and Paul, and I managed to do our job without much fuss.

The Wild Bunch – I'm fourth from left.

The Miller Brothers.

Howzat! – l to r. Whiz, Paul, Graham (bat), Ronnie, Ken, Terry.

A Night in Manhattans – l to r. Bob, Tommy, Linda, Terry and Mickey.

Hard at it.

A pair of bouncers.

The In-laws and the Out-laws – l to r. Ronnie, Kathy, Terry, Linda, Richard and Evelyn.

Family portrait.

Camping in France.

Holiday in Yarmouth

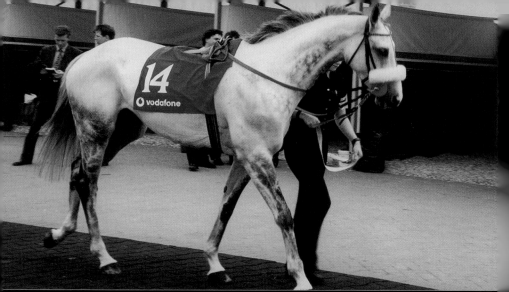

Pendle in her prime

Linda receiving the Thirsk Hunt Cup.

The winning team – l to r. Terry, Alex, Dandy, Linda and Julie.

CHAPTER SEVEN

WEDDING BELLS AND ROBBERY HELL

A t twenty-one I got married for the first time and it was something I should never have done. At that age, divorce is inevitable and mine came after six months. She wasn't the best person for me to marry but I was young and I think it was the idea of being married which appealed to me rather than being in love.

We didn't try very hard at the marriage and I certainly wasn't committed to the woman. Neither of us was better than the other. I was messing around in Newcastle, getting drunk and seeing as many women as I could. Someone told me after a while that she had got sick of her life and was seeing other men too.

At that age we were too young for the responsibility and just wanted to have fun, which is exactly what we did until the inevitable parting of the ways.

On the day of my wedding, my father actually wept because he didn't want me to marry her. In fact, he encouraged me not to go to the wedding right up to the last minute. His concern was that I was too young to be married and he had nothing against the woman personally, he could see his son making a huge mistake so he just wanted me to have every chance to avoid it.

Being engaged and married meant absolutely nothing to me at that time. I can't think of anything more boring than shopping for rings. To me it's as exciting as watching paint dry. In my opinion, most men do it to keep their women happy, not because it appeals to them.

The marriage only lasted six months but that was enough time for us both to know that it was never going to work. To make matters worse, we took a flat at Longbenton, not far away from my mam's house and I have to say that I missed living at home a hell of a lot. It's a lot harder for men to fly the nest than it is for women and I was having a very bad time adjusting to the responsibility of a new wife and my own home, so I thought that going home would be going back to my previous life there when we split up.

My mother was delighted when I moved back home but she never let me know that. It was a blessing in disguise when I went back because around this time my mates and I were made redundant from the Tarmac laying company.

As soon as I moved back into my mam's house I knew something was different; it wasn't the house that had changed but me. I felt uncomfortable about being there and I realised my independence was gone. In my own home I could do anything I wanted, eat when I wanted and live the life I chose, but now I felt worried about taking something from the fridge or turning the T.V. over to watch something I wanted to see. The bedrooms had to be disrupted to accommodate me too, they moved me in with my brother

William and I'm sure he wasn't pleased about that.

Having a night out with my mates put a further burden on the family when I would come home at three in the morning, knocking my dad up to let me in. The poor bloke used to work a three shift pattern on 2pm – 10pm, 6am – 2pm or 10pm - 6am but I was a thoughtless git who didn't think twice about what shift he was working when I needed to be back in the house. I would regularly make a nuisance of myself because of the thoughtless way I was carrying on.

My mam must have been a really special person then, she had to deal with women's problems working at the ministry and then come home to wash, clean and cook for all of us at home. It must have been a hell of a feat to fit it all in with little or no time for herself.

There is nothing more degrading than being on the dole, it was one of the most embarrassing times of my life. The Government doesn't realise that no matter how much they tart their dole offices up, it's the feeling inside you that you're discarded and written off which matters.

The members of the gangs talked about the redundancy packages we would get but we all knew it wouldn't last long. Some of them started up their own businesses because they couldn't stand the thought of being on the dole. Others got jobs with alternative road laying firms and I was offered a job with another company too. I refused it because I was just sick and tired of the drinking associated with the industry.

The gym work I was doing took up a lot of time and I was progressing nicely. I knew the drinking was hindering my development so I didn't want to stay in the profession.

One of my biggest regrets is that I didn't keep in contact with some of the lads who I worked with at that time. A couple of them died, including old Joe and I wish someone had contacted me when it happened as I loved that old man.

Brian always used to call me his son and I heard that his real boy had eventually taken my position on the road gang, A few years ago, I read in the local paper that Brian and his lad had been having a big drinking session in a local pub when the son collapsed and died. It was just one of life's tragic occurrences. I know a lot of people will say that it was a stupid thing to do but that doesn't help the people who are left. When I was young I could party with the best. My body was attuned for it but today I am satisfied with a couple of pints and the T.V. usually.

At this stage of my life I was only interested in sex and drink and I partook of copious amounts of both. The number of times I woke up with a thumping head, next to a woman whose name I couldn't even remember, gave my mates some great laughs but if the truth was really known, I wasn't happy. I was going through the motions of being one of the lads, which was fair enough I suppose, but in the end my lifestyle just sickened me.

Leaving a woman's house in Gateshead on a freezing cold morning with the rain pissing down on my head, depressed me a hell of a lot. I felt dirty, ashamed and depressed. I needed a steadying influence and I was fortunate to get it.

It was while I was working on the doors that I met my wife, Linda. She was a bit older than me but I thought she was exciting from the moment I met her. A few months after we met, I had the rare opportunity of a weekend off from the bouncing business so we decided to have a night out on the town. When we got there, I ran into Scotty, my boss from the Bigg Market clubs, and he asked me to do him a favour because he was short of bodies for the night. As long as Linda could stand with me, I told him I would do it and it was so funny an hour later watching Linda stopping blokes with tattoos and turning away anyone she didn't like the look of.

She was revelling in the power when the buzzer sounded. I told her I had to go but to stay where she was and be careful. When I got to the scene two lads were going at it hammer and tongs so I got in between them, pushing one of them away.

The two girls with them didn't like that one bit and started to kick off themselves. Suddenly Linda appeared from nowhere grabbing one, telling her to get out or she would throw her out. It was at this point the two girls made a disastrous decision and jumped Linda. Three seconds later it was all over, she had laid them out and had them up and ejected before they knew what was happening.

Scotty arrived, laughing his head off as the women hit the street, asking Linda if she wanted my job.

Linda and I were married on the 27th August, 1988. It was a really lovely day all round, the weather was perfect and everyone had a great time. It was literally the best day of my life and I have thought that everyday of the eighteen years we have been together.

There was a problem though and no wedding is complete without one. As the best man and I dressed for the occasion, we were mortified to find the suits didn't fit. We had ordered them and given our sizes but with two hours to go we looked like Bill and Ben. Buttons were missing, sleeves were too short and the hire shop was thirty minutes away.

When we arrived at the hire shop it got worse. They didn't have any replacements in stock and it ended up with the assistant stripping the dummies in the window to find us the right sizes. There we were in the middle of the floor in an upmarket hire shop taking the first trousers off and dressing in the new kit. It gave the best man a cracking speech.

In fact, I still think Linda is perfect and the sexiest woman I have ever met. She has that indefinable quality that I just love. She knows how to be a wife, lover and friend and not every man gets a woman like that. I'm lucky, but then again so is she as I am a bit of a romantic stud when the occasion calls for it. She might disagree, but I am entitled to dream.

She had just been divorced from her first husband and I'm pleased I never met him in those days. I was jealous to the point of madness and I don't think a meeting between us would have been very constructive. It seems that the moment I turned thirty the envy left me and I'm very pleased about that.

I think it's fair to say that Linda's mother was worried about who she was going out with after her divorce, I remember her looking at Linda with that suspicious expression most mothers have over their daughter's boyfriends.

Linda's mam had some plastering work to be done which a friend of mine and I agreed to do. We asked her to buy us some 18 hole Doctor Martin boots as payment. It was a joke but she took it seriously and got them for us. My mate and I had a good laugh as we put them on, telling her we were skinheads. I'm sure it was that which made her suspicious of us. The moment Linda's dad set eyes on me he said, "By God Linda, you really know how to pick the rough ones".

Linda was incredible. As I said, I had discovered women some time before but they always seemed to be the type who were happy to let the man lead them in everything. People might be a bit surprised at this but I am the kind of bloke who is happy for a lady to be as strong a character as myself.

Our first date showed me that I had made an excellent choice in asking Linda out. Her car broke down on a filthy night and she took over the situation completely. I sat in the front of the car as she took out a hammer and opened the bonnet. A few well-directed blows freed the stuck starter motor and I hadn't even had to leave the warm interior of the car. Now that's what I call a practical woman, she really swept me off my feet.

It didn't end there. The dual carriageway where we had stopped was a very busy road in Newcastle and Linda spotted a milk float trundling down the three lane road on the other side of the crash barrier. She dashed over the busy road and stopped the milk float to buy me a bottle of milk. What a woman!

We lived together for a while before marrying but I reckon that first date decided my mind, this was the woman for me. I've given all you middle-aged single girls the secret with that story, now go out and get your man.

My first real catering experience came through Linda's family. Her brother was renovating a derelict pub, converting it to a restaurant in Stamfordham and I helped him bring the place up to scratch. When it was done, we decided to open it ourselves and began putting on basic fare for the customers.

It was a fantastic fifteen years but eventually we were receiving lots of enquiries about outside catering jobs and so we opened my other business, Millers Catering. Looking back over the years, my school training and Newcastle Polytechnic was invaluable in giving me the grounding in basic food. It helped so much when the restaurant was in full flow.

It could have been so different because I almost got expelled from college for spilling something (I can't remember what after all these years) into a vat which contained £50 worth of chocolate and completely ruining it. I told the staff it was an accident and that saved my bacon. After all these years I think I can finally admit that it was no such thing. Boys will be boys.

My mother is still alive and going strong and it was while I was running the pub with Linda, that my father unfortunately had a stroke and it affected him very badly. It got so distressing that I couldn't visit him for a long time. If I'm honest about it, I was scared to death. The last thing you want to see is one of your parents in that state. As strokes go, it was a bad one. It robbed him of his speech and faculties.

I've never felt as helpless as I did then. I don't mind admitting I cried buckets at that time. He was bedridden for three years and it was a terrible thing to see him deteriorate.

As time went on, it was evident he wasn't going to survive and Linda (the rock of my life) told me I had to conquer my fear and see him. I'm so pleased I did. He was a plain man with a plain life. Work, regular visits to the pub to see his mates and short holidays with my mother were the extent of his life but I'll tell you something, he loved all of it. He once said that if he had won the lottery, he would hire a driver to take him to the pub, that was the limit of his ambition. I'm sure there are many people who have tragedy in their lives and have to cope with appalling situations but this was another point of my mother's life which I thought highly of her for. She handled it all with dignity.

My father would have been so proud of me for starting my own business and winning Hell's Kitchen but mostly for owning my own racehorse and winning on T.V. A flutter was one of his favourite pastimes.

I love my horses and all animals. I'm a cat lover now and they are the perfect creatures to relieve the kind of tension I feel in my work. I just love the furry little bundles.

It began with a wild cat which used to visit the pub and it had the most enormous face I've ever seen, it was the size of a dinner plate. If that cat's eyes were in the middle of the road you would have seen them from space, they were so big.

The number of times that cat got me into trouble with Linda is amazing. It had a particular liking for king prawns and chicken and I indulged its tastes. That animal ate better food than most of my customers and certainly better than I ever have. Linda would look at the cost of the food devoted to the cat and predict it was either her or the animal. There was no contest but I never told her that I left food all over the outside areas so it wouldn't starve.

I am an animal lover in general. Despite the fact that I am a chef, I can't to this day put a lobster into boiling water, I leave that to one of my other chefs to do. One of the most horrific things I have ever seen is the killing process in the abattoir and I will never watch that again as long as I live. On the day I was there, I watched a cow and two sheep slaughtered and it still gives me nightmares today.

In fact, the whole slaughtering situation has given me problems to this day and there are other things which sicken me too. Veal crating and battery chicken houses are others which make me seethe. How we can treat animals like that is beyond me and take it from me, I'm sure an animal knows when it's about to be slaughtered, the squeals are like nothing you've ever heard on the worst horror movie you've ever seen and the loosing of the faecal matter and urine is a horrific sight.

One afternoon I arrived home from the gym to find Linda sitting in the restaurant between two burly men. She looked terrified as she introduced them as two policemen. Around this time there were a spate of robberies happening at pubs and clubs in the North East. Apparently we were next on the list and the police advised us that we were due to be robbed the following Sunday. Their intelligence unit had discovered that two particularly unsavoury and violent characters had marked us out for their next job and they weren't averse to using shotguns. Linda and me are no shy violets but I can tell you that we have never been so terrified in all our lives as we were that week.

We were advised to have the children looked after elsewhere so we sent them to Linda's mothers. It caused us a lot of soul searching when we discovered that the youngsters thought we didn't want them anymore. That's the way kids of that age think I suppose when their life is turned upside down.

When I found out the whole story it was even more worrying. The robbers had been watching me lock up the place night after night from fields opposite the pub. They were going to overpower me, put a shotgun to my head and force me to open the safe. When someone tells you that armed robbers have been stalking you, the feeling is indescribable. Fear makes you sick to the stomach and the fact of being helpless against these thugs takes over your life. The will to survive takes over and all I wanted to do was get these people first and make them feel how Linda and I felt. I was quite prepared to take the consequences if I got my hands on them.

The police noticed the state we were in and gave us two policemen to live on the premises with us as protection, but I don't mind admitting now that I couldn't sleep and spent nights sitting near the main pub door, armed with a baseball bat and my brother-in-law's shotgun under the seat. I was taking no chance of us being hurt. If anything happened I would be the same as Tony Martin. Whoever was coming into my house to hurt me or any of my family, I would make sure I got them first and I see nothing wrong with that.

Day after day, Linda and I had to go about our work with this over our heads. We had to appear as normal as possible to staff and customers alike and it wasn't easy. I couldn't concentrate on the job in hand so I am sure that my cooking that week wasn't up to scratch, but we got through it.

On the Sunday when the robbery was due to take place, a brewery lorry turned up. Instead of the usual kegs and alcopops, twenty six officers dressed from head to foot in black, complete with masks and weapons leapt from the interior. It looked like the SAS had arrived on a major terrorist incident. They crashed into the pub and checked every nook and cranny. If they had only asked, I would have told them that no one was lurking there.

The authorities had set up lights everywhere and, thinking they would come in through the living room, they erected three sets above each of the patio doors. It looked like a TV studio with equipment and tripod lights all over the place. They wanted us to be normal they said and we did our best but my backside was working overtime.

That was the longest night of my entire life and as I looked out I saw a bloke wandering around outside with a strange device on his back. They had set up a radio with a secure channel so that the robbers couldn't listen in. All night we kept hearing that they were on their way and it wouldn't be long but they never did turn up.

At eight the next morning the brewery wagon turned up again and they all left with the main policeman telling us that there was no need to worry because they knew who they were and had sent a car to see the robbers and tell them they knew what they were up to. They sent a bloke around to install a panic button and that was it, Linda and I were on our own. We were in shock but had to move on and it was a Godsend that we got past that.

As it turned out, nothing ever happened but that was the end of our tenure of the pub. We decided to get out.

CHAPTER EIGHT

FAMILY

No matter which way you look at it, the only people you can really trust in this life are the members of your family and sometimes you can't even trust members who aren't the closest in the family circle. I'm really lucky in that respect, to have close relations who are really supportive but who will tell me honestly if they think I'm wrong.

My two sons, Graeme and Anthony, are poles apart as characters. Graeme works with me as bar manager in my restaurant, while Anthony is a talented chef and we have worked together in the kitchen a lot in the past.

Anthony wanted to get involved in work from a very early age and started with me at thirteen years old. It really pleased me because I love the idea of kids getting used to the work ethic early. Earning their own money and getting used to looking after cash at that age is a great way of learning responsibility. It never put him off doing the most mundane jobs, like peeling onions and prepping in general.

In some ways, I wonder if giving him the really basic tasks was my way of trying to put him off the business but if that was my idea it certainly didn't work, he just worked and worked to make as much money as he could.

He is a fantastic artist too and could have been an outstanding graphic designer but it wasn't to be. He got involved in some stupid, childish things which most kids do. Unfortunately, he started to get mixed up in setting fire to fields so I told him, if he wanted to play with fire he needed to get into the kitchen, and he did.

He was lucky that I could bring him into the business to work and give him a focus. The lads all took to him from the first minute, having a laugh with him, making sure he felt that he was part of the environment. I put him on dishwashing to begin with, starting to train him in cooking at the same time. After a while he progressed to commis chef, getting to the point where he could tell me to have a night off while he did all the cooking. It all seemed to be going well and then there was a massive setback.

There is no easy way to say this so I'll just put it down cold on this paper, Anthony is presently serving a prison term for an offence he committed some time ago. Most parents will tell you that it's a mistake that their offspring are in prison but my entire family know that Anthony's offence was committed and most importantly, Anthony himself realises the gravity of what he did and accepts the fact that he should pay the penalty for his crime. All the boy wants now is to finish his time and get back to work with me as soon as possible.

Being in prison has shown him a life of restriction, along with living in a state of no privacy and he hates the fact.

When Anthony did what he did and was sentenced, it put a massive strain on the rest of the family, which is understandable. The shock of dealing with a Crown Court trial inevitably caused problems between me and Linda. Over the years there have been highs and lows and it could have caused a marital break up but thankfully we are still together. It won't be long now until he is released, which we can't wait to happen.

When he finally gets out, the whole family has decided that he will never go back. We will be there for him twenty-four hours a day and he knows that this is the one chance he has to rehabilitate himself with our help. If he makes a pig's ear of it, he will have to suffer the consequences. As a family we aren't being hard, we just want to make sure one of our own never has to go through the degradation of prison again. I really feel for Linda in all this, she's a mother who blames herself for her son's sin and I keep telling her that she can't take on her son's wrongdoing. Linda has always supported me in everything throughout the years and this was one occasion when she depended on me for support, which I was so pleased I could give.

From the moment I met Linda we were soul mates. I could have searched a thousand years and never found anyone so in tune with me. She is a little older than me but I'm not going to say how much because I have to sleep next to her and she may do a John Bobbit on me if I do.

It was Linda who was the driving force behind us getting into business in the first place and I am eternally grateful for her confidence in me. That kind of belief gave me the drive I needed to make a success of my work. She has never wavered in her faith and I hope I've paid her back for it.

She is some business woman too, diners feel really special when she welcomes them in her front of house role. I have never seen anyone with as much feeling for the job. It's not unusual for her to offer the diners her glasses if they can't read the menu. I am the worrier of the two of us but she is the most focused person. She knows what she needs to do in business and when to do it, which leaves me free for my main task of cooking. At the risk of repeating myself earlier in the book, she is the sexiest woman in the world. No matter how long we have been married, she still turns me on like no woman ever has. I'll bet there are a lot of marriages where the passion died after the first few years but that hasn't happened in ours and long may it remain.

I keep telling her I am a bit of a stud and she keeps telling me to dream on. It's probably her way to keep me on my toes and it works. If you're happy at home there is no reason to look elsewhere and I am delirious at home so she has no worry on that score. Oh, and she thinks she is a better cook than I am, but I just let her delude herself regarding that. In fact, I have a Yorkshire pudding that Linda made on my fireplace in the kitchen, which is little and flat. Where the rising agent went I've no idea but when we argue about cooking I pick it up and hold it up to her face just smiling and she hates it.

She's had a lot of problems to contend with in life and she has borne them all with more strength and courage than anyone has a right to have. Her brother Ronny, died when Linda was fifteen and she still talks about having to go to the lead works to tell her dad what had happened and the trembling she felt along the way.

Her daughter, Julie, was involved in a very serious car

accident a few years ago. We almost lost her, the head injuries she received were massive and the doctors didn't give her much hope of survival. Julie was, and still is, a beautiful girl but her personality was changed by the event. It's hard to come to terms with it as she wasn't driving, somehow you feel that, if she was behind the wheel, it is more acceptable but when someone else was the cause, it hits home pretty hard.

The accident occurred in Doncaster too. Imagine how we felt to be contacted at four in the morning to tell us that news, it was devastating. The long drive to Yorkshire through the night gave us plenty of time to think the worst.

I've never felt so helpless as when I saw Julie for the first time following the accident, it just cut me up so badly. Linda was in pieces when she saw the plight of her daughter. There's nothing like a loved one in an intensive care bed to scare the hell out of you. Tubes and monitors are everywhere, with all the terrifying sounds of the machines breaking the silence of the room. It isn't designed to worry you but by Christ it does.

All I could do in that situation was hug Linda and tell her everything would be ok, when if I'm honest, I was as petrified as she was. Looking down at the unconscious form of Julie made me realise how flimsy the hold on life really is. I don't want to lecture anyone but I would say to any joyrider, think before you get behind that wheel. Don't think about yourself because you've already decided what you are about to do, think about your family and in particular your mother. If you die, you'll leave her to a life of regret and guilt that will haunt her till the day she dies.

Julie wasn't a joyrider and she wasn't driving the car in which she had the accident. That shows how an ordinary accident can devastate many lives and a joyrider will go out with the intention of driving at suicidal speeds and recklessly. What exactly do they think might happen?

It took Julie a long tortuous time to get out of hospital, the doctors fought to save her life and in the end won, but it could have been so, so different.

Ever since that day, Julie has battled against her injuries and the war goes on. It will probably last the rest of her life but she is like her mother, with the same steely determination to beat the odds so I know she will do it. We are so proud of her as a family. She's now the partner of Billy Hardy the ex boxer and they have given Linda and myself a beautiful grandson, Will. He is only nine months old as I write this but already you can see the determination in his character that Julie and Linda have.

Julie has a fight on her hands for any compensation from the car smash. It drives me insane when I think of the time it is taking for her to be compensated for an accident she had no responsibility for. That's government for you, they will spend billions on defence but ignore someone who is incapacitated. It doesn't matter which party is in power, they have more feeling for how they are regarded as politicians in the rest of the world, rather than do what is right for someone who has been physically injured in their own land.

My son Graeme was particularly upset about what happened to his sister. As I said earlier, he has a very different personality to his brother, a much deeper thinker who considers the implications of everything before he gets involved. Out of the two boys, I feel Graeme would be the more likely to be a businessman, he just seems to have that deep instinct and a wickedly dry sense of humour, who doesn't suffer fools gladly.

As a young lad he became fascinated with machinery and that interest has stayed with him to this day. At five or six he asked us for a tool box and at ten he wanted a chain saw. It was so funny to watch the salesman trying to sell it to us, when Graeme knew more about the equipment than he did. I bet he gave a huge sigh of relief when he saw the back of us. His face was a picture when Graeme asked him technical questions which he struggled to answer.

When Graeme was about three years old and I was involved in building, he would constantly be on my back asking to come with me and work with his dad. I would tether him to me and let him work alongside, doing proper jobs. He was happy as a pig in muck about that. That's where he got his love for machinery, so I've no one to blame but myself for that.

It got to the point when he reached school age, where he wanted to come with me rather than go to school and I used to have to lie to him, telling him that I wasn't going to work that day just to get him to the school gates.

In some ways, I'm surprised Graeme didn't go into a more technical profession. Don't get me wrong, I am delighted he is working with me and he is an excellent bar manager but I thought he might want to work with the machinery he loves so much. For anyone who saw Hell's Kitchen, Graeme was the one who ran down, kissing and cuddling me when I won.

We fight like cat and dog both at work and at home but there is the kind of devotion that family members should have between them. There isn't one family in the land where the members get on all the time. He's a little sod when he winds me up and he knows exactly how to set me off. When the fireworks fly between us it gets a bit loud and basic but it all goes right in the restaurant in the end.

There are the great times too, when we spend nights just talking and laughing at the stupidest things and I love those times. The trouble between Graeme and myself stems from our characters, we're both too stubborn to give way in an argument and that can cause problems. It gets a bit fraught when we are going at it hammer and tongs and Linda comes to put her views into the conversation. The lads in the kitchen have seen it all before and they just get their heads down and carry on with the work.

I've talked a bit about my mam in the early part of the book, so you know that in many ways she's had a hard life but she wouldn't say it was any harder than many of the others who grew up alongside her.

My brothers are a good example of Geordie lads. As I've said, I have five of them. Our John has worked for the Post Office since he left school, Richard and George for the local council, wor Ronnie is a park warden and William has not worked for a while due to long term illness.

Those are real people. People who struggle to exist and have never had the chance to rise above their station in life, but they are honest and hard working men, like most of the wonderful people from the North East. That's why we have a reputation of being a friendly nation.

Family is highly important to me. When all is said and done, they are the only ones who will be there for you through the good and bad and that is how it should be.

CHAPTER NINE

WORST TIME OF MY LIFE

My father and I were always very close but following his stroke he was very poorly for a long time. During his illness, my brothers Richard and William were still at home and helped my mother through the really hard times of my dad's sickness, fetching and carrying for her and generally giving her the support she needed.

I visited him periodically over the years but he had slowly deteriorated each time I saw him. For a man who had been active all his life, even if it was just a walk to the pub, it was terrible to see and my heart bled for him.

One day I turned up at the house and noticed his face and neck were covered in acne, which was too severe to be just a small outbreak. I took one look at him and knew that there was something drastically wrong. My mother didn't look too great either, due to the constant care she was giving him.

I asked how long he had been in this state and she told me a couple of months. The scary part was that she also told me he had been howling at nights, like a wolf, and she wasn't getting much sleep. At that moment, I knew had to do something about his condition and I blamed myself for not seeing him on a regular basis.

My dad was being tended by the District Nurse for bed sores once a week and she told my mam that it was sometimes normal for people to get acne when they had an allergic reaction to their medication. I knew different and phoned the doctors straight away. As I spoke to him on the other end of the phone, I wasn't very happy because he seemed unconcerned. He actually told me that, if he had to come out to every sixty-five-year-old patient suffering from acne he wouldn't get round them in a month. It wasn't really the acne that I was concerned about to be honest. It was a sixth sense kicking in and I just knew something was seriously wrong. I knew he needed urgent medical attention. An awful feeling came over me that he wasn't going to make it. To give the doctor his due, he did say he would call on his rounds but after two days of sheer hell for my father, I wondered which round on which week he meant. Taking one look at my dad when he got there, the doctor called an ambulance immediately. It's a good job he did call the ambulance because they discovered he was suffering from gangrene at the hospital and amputated his leg the next day. The howling was the only way the poor man could let us know how much pain he was feeling.

I really believe that my father never knew they had taken off his leg because the brain damage from the stroke was so severe. That is just my impression, but I do know he must have suffered in pain for months and had no way of telling anyone.

One thing I have always been concerned about is a

District Nurse dressing a patient's leg that is suffering with a condition like that and not noticing it, it's beyond me.

I have never felt the level of guilt before or since, that I endured at that time. Prior to this, it had been two months since I last saw him and there is no excuse in the world for that. I only hope that wherever he is, he can forgive me for it.

When I visited him in hospital he looked settled and my mam seemed to be benefiting from the rest of not being a constant carer. The toll it had taken on her was awful. She looked washed out and older than her years.

He had been hospitalised for a while but was in a stable condition, when there came the day that Linda turned to me and told me I should see my dad that day because my mam had been on the phone. I had been using the saying that it's better to remember the way they were in good health than seeing them when they are in the state of poor health, as an excuse for staying away.

In all honesty, I think I wasn't man enough to face up to seeing him coming to the closing moments of his life.

When I got to the hospital and saw my brothers there, I knew that it was very serious. My mother looked terrible, she had been there a week and I thought she needed some time away from the situation. She only lived a couple of miles from the hospital and it was about 10am when I arrived. He seemed OK so about noon, I told her to come home with me for an hour for a cup of tea and have some fish and chips. I'm sure the others would have done it but I was the only one who could drive and had a car. I thought it would do her good.

When we got there I ran along to the fish shop and made a cup of tea for her when I got back. We hadn't been there ten minutes when the phone rang and it was my brother Ronny. He just said, "You better come back, he's dead".

The icy fingers of dread which crept up my spine seemed to be clutching the breath out of me. I told my mother and I'll never forget the look on her face, she had missed his death and I knew it was my fault. Words can't describe how I felt at that moment, losing the best person I had ever loved and depriving my mother of her last moments with the man she had spent her life with.

When we got to the hospital, she asked my brothers if he had opened his eyes and they all said yes, she just broke down and sobbed her heart out.

At that moment, I knew how much it had meant to her that he had looked his last into her eyes and I had destroyed all that. I'd destroyed it with ignorance and stupidity and there was no way I could make it better.

My father had always told me throughout his life that when he died he wanted two things to happen; one was he didn't want me to cry because he had a good life (sorry dad, I failed on that one) and two was that I was to have a good drink for him (I managed that one dad).

It was the first death I'd been involved with and I really hadn't taken it as seriously as the others because of my inexperience of the situation. That's where I slipped up and to this day, I will never forgive myself for that fact.

My mother's first reaction had done that to me. Afterwards she told me that not being there was probably for the best but she was a mother just consoling her son. On that awful day I cried every hour, I had a pain in the front of my head which I've never had since. There was no way to get rid of it. My mother gave me a glass of sherry and half a bottle later, the pain eased a bit. I remembered my dad's instruction about having a drink on him and I had broken his first wish so I wasn't going to break this one.

My brothers and I went to the Cradlewell and Corner House pubs and we got into that cycle of drinking while talking about the deceased and what he would be thinking now. Sometimes alcohol is a good thing. The drink was flowing freely and we got into an argument when a scuffle broke out between me and my oldest brother, Richard.

The pair of us have always got on well but when he has a drink he works himself. As a result of the scuffle I fell over, turning my ankle badly. It was the worst sprain I have ever had and I was forced to attend the funeral on crutches.

As I sat in the church at Heaton Cemetery in Newcastle listening to his favourite Frank Sinatra records, it was heart wrenching. It was a week later and I was still inconsolable.

He had a dignified send off, one which anyone would have been proud of. When John and I had visited the funeral home to pick out a coffin we asked for the best and most expensive one. Most funeral directors would have taken the money and run but the man who dealt with us could see how upset we were and calmed me down, telling us that they had some reasonably priced caskets which were more than adequate and we could consider picking one of those.

He was right in the end. I was just trying to portray an image of having plenty of money and my dad would have hated that. I could think of the times when I had a few quid in my back pocket and could have given him some but didn't and the times when I had driven past the house, going God knows where and didn't call in. Death brings all your transgressions back to you.

From the moment of his death to now, I have tortured myself about my treatment of him before he died. Linda has to regularly pull me together but I still have the memories of my dad sitting next to me in front of the coal fire he had lit at 6.30am with a bacon sandwich and a cup of tea when I was young. I would run into that front room freezing cold from my bedroom upstairs and see his smiling face first thing in the morning. No one can take those memories from me.

On a Saturday afternoon, Linda and I would sit with him at the local and I would tell him about my antics on the Friday night. He would laugh his head off at me and have the biggest grin in the world on his features.

Each year on his birthday, my brother John goes to the grave and pours a bottle of whisky over it. I never knew that he had asked John to do that. God, I miss him so much.

CHAPTER TEN

GEORDIELAND

I am a Geordie first, an Englishman second and British in the third instance. That's just how it is, being born and bred in Newcastle Upon Tyne. There aren't enough words or phrases to explain how I feel about the North East, to get over my passion for the area. If there is a more beautiful part of the world, I haven't seen it and as far as the people go, I defy anyone to tell me there are friendlier folk than the Geordies. Where else in this land could you be a stranger and have someone buy you a drink just because you're a visitor?

I'm very much a traditional Englishman where food is concerned and that's because I genuinely feel our fare stands up favourably against all the so-called superior cuisine of the world. A traditional Sunday roast or steak and kidney pie is better in my view than frogs' legs or sauerkraut.

The North East has some wonderful areas to see, including a world heritage site in Hadrian's Wall, incomparable beaches and so many castles with ancient pasts, it's untrue.

Bamburgh, Dunstanburgh, Alnwick, Warkworth, Chillingham or Holy Island, every one of those castles has a proud and interesting history which is important to the country's heritage. Those aren't the only castles in Northumbria but one of my favourites has to be Bamburgh, which is set on the coast of the North part of the region and has been seen or featured in major films like Elizabeth with Cate Blanchett. It looks out to sea on an imposing hill and is above a wild rocky area and sandy beach with grassy dunes above. The beauty of it is breathtaking.

One of the favourite pastimes of Geordies is fishing. We live quite close to the sea so a spot of sea fishing is a relaxing occupation in this hurly burly world of stress and speed. I used to love watching the fishing fleets, straining with laden catches, offload at North Shields and, until fishing quotas were brought in, the catches were some of the best in the country. In 2006, I went to the port one day to see the catch come in and it was nothing to speak of, just a few forlorn boxes on the quayside. In my heart, I feel so sorry for the fishing industry up here, they've gone from a vibrant business, to not even a shadow of its former self. The industry has been decimated and a lot of brave, dedicated men have lost their livelihoods. How could we let that happen? When I looked at the dock, it was the same size as it always was, the only things missing were the boats and the banter. My kids used to love to go there to smell the smells and see the work and one of them asked a fisherman to give him a fish so he could take it home and tell his mam he caught it. The bloke selected the biggest fish he had, an absolutely magnificent North Sea cod and passed it over for free. That fish would cost £20 in today's prices. That's the stamp of the people here.

Just North of North Shields we have the coastal resorts of Tynemouth, Whitley Bay and Cullercoats and each have magnificent beaches. In the past, they were frequented by hoards of Scots down on their summer holidays but today Whitley Bay is a hen and stag party area and the family charm has gone.

Empty and boarded up amusement arcades look forlorn while waiting for demolition which saddens me, as I loved putting an old penny in them as a child to win two pennies back. They've made way for flats and unattractive car parks now, but the stretches of golden sand in front of these makes up for the change on the land.

The coastal route North is filled with other interesting and beautiful villages like Blyth, Newbiggin By The Sea and Amble but it's when you get to Craster that you get a feel of the kind of food we can produce.

Craster kippers are famous the world over and I love the odd kipper for breakfast. They have a distinctive curing process and smoke house which makes their produce much sought after. It's a tiny olde worlde village with a few pubs and restaurants and two picturesque harbours.

Alnwick, is a bit South of Craster and has a yearly food festival in which the locals bring their own produce to show and sell, from meat to simple ice cream. I have a bit of a moan about markets and food festivals in general. In my view, the owners should allow plenty of free tasting so that people can judge for themselves whether to buy, but whenever you go to these things it's always buy without trying. Would you buy a car without a test drive? No, and you shouldn't be asked to buy food before trying it either.

In 2006, I attended the festival and made some nettle soup for the people. It was a really excellent day in a wonderful setting. If you've ever watched the start of the first series of Blackadder you will see the silhouette of Alnwick Castle,the home of the Percy family. It is one of the most important fortifications in England with a history second to none.

Part of the festival is a nettle recipe competition which I take part in. The old wives tale says that, if you have nettles three times in the month of May you'll never be ill for the rest of the year. They also say there is a way of picking nettles by hand without stinging but I've always given that part a miss.

The wife of the present Duke of Northumberland, who owns the castle, has established an imposing and impressive new garden within the Duke's property. It's a modern feature but in-keeping with the local town and area. Alnwick is a place where you can really step back in time.

In the West of Northumbria we have a rich vein of Roman towns set up in the shadow of Hadrian's Wall, like Hexham and Corbridge. Sometimes we take the wall for granted living here, which is pretty dreadful but I suppose when you live as close to something as historically significant, you sometimes forget how important to the world it really is.

My brother John was going to China on holiday and was looking forward to seeing the Great Wall there but when I asked him about Hadrian's Wall, he admitted he had never seen it. See what I mean?

In all of the towns and villages that I've mentioned, it's possible to buy some of the most amazing local produce but most people still go to the supermarket for everything. Try local specialist cheeses or butcher provided meat and sausage and taste the difference, yes it will cost a bit more but I promise you that the difference is well worth a few extra pence.

Hexham is a good example of local shops which are choc-full of the most amazing foods. These local shopkeepers try desperately to provide high quality produce at a reasonable cost and if we want them to survive, all of us must buy some of our weekly groceries in these shops, even buying one item a week would be a massive help to the traders. I just love these places, with real experts serving you the best and I hope they never die.

Think about shopping in areas still unspoiled with cobbled streets, superb market squares, back street antique shops and real people serving, isn't that better than a plastic supermarket? I am not being hypocritical because I buy oysters locally and get boudain noir, boudain blanc, various flavour sausage, wild salmon, fresh herbs and game from these places and will continue to do it. At the last market I attended, I bought some nettle cordial. Putting it behind the bar I made a drink of vodka, nettle and lemonade which flew out. People loved it.

Working men's clubs are an important part of life up here, where flower and leek shows give a good element of competition to gardeners. They will labour all year round to produce the most amazing blooms and vegetables which have to be seen to be believed.

Over the city and town areas, you will see the sky filled with hundreds of racing pigeons. Make no mistake, it is a sport and a lucrative one at that. The money which is won by the best birds is not to be sniffed at. Most of the fanciers will tell you that it isn't the money that's important, they really love training their birds to beat rival pigeons.

In the working men's clubs, I've catered for all of these dedicated blokes and they all possess a real individual character. The officials who run the clubs stand out in a crowd. One guy I used to see in the local club had a nose three times its normal size and it was all due to the drink but that doesn't mean he is a bad person.

From my own point of view, I was so lucky to find my restaurant between St. Nicholas Cathedral and the Castle Keep. The keep has been in Newcastle for hundreds of years, right in the city centre, but you could miss it if you weren't looking for it.

At one time, Ashington in Northumberland was the biggest mining village in Europe. That was until Maggie decided the pits were surplus to requirements of course.

Now a proud mining industry has been decimated by government policy and I think that the politicians wanted these areas to be ghost towns. The men had shown the gall to try and fight for their jobs as the miners did all around the land and Maggie didn't like that one little bit. She can say what she likes about needing to modernise our fuel policy but I will always believe she did it all through sheer bloody mindedness, that's no way to govern a people. The trouble was she didn't get her wish because the Geordies and Northumbrians fought back to keep their communities alive.

New types of work and industry have sprung up and we're now showing what we can do, even though they tried to grind us into the dirt.

If you look at it logically, we've lost our two main industries here in fishing and mining and law and order has inevitably broken down. So you tell me, if we had still been allowed the dignity of work through these industries, would there be as much violence and robbery today? I don't think there would.

Some wonderful food came out of the mining and fishing villages of Northumbria too, stews with dumplings, leek puddings, mince and dumplings and all kinds of other fantastic dishes. Those things will never die up here.

I hope you will understand my reasons for putting in a chapter about my beloved Geordieland with all the area's fantastic advantages but there is one place I have to mention here before I go and that is the hallowed cathedral that is St. James' Park. If you want an illustration of the character of a people, look at the supporters of Newcastle United. No domestic trophy since 1955 and one major European trophy in 1969 and yet 52,000 go to worship every week, just in the hope we will do it this year. It's impossible to get in on a normal basis and if we were winning major competitions regularly, we would get 80,000 minimum with a further development of the ground.

Big Al has to be mentioned here in the same breath as St. James'. On his testimonial evening there was a full house, 52,000 for a testimonial. Can you imagine that happening anywhere else in the world? Even the big man was struggling when a full house of Geordies started twirling their scarves around their heads. You've know idea how we are going to miss you, big man. You are a God and Newcastle should be run to the gospel of Saint Alan.

CHAPTER ELEVEN

DIETS-R-ME

I've just had a shower and am sitting on the edge of the bed trying to pull my socks on but it's a real effort. I turn to Linda and tell her I'm starting a diet today. Her face shows the boring realisation of another fair-weather promise and she says, "Terry, what happened to last Monday's diet and the Monday before that diet and the Monday before that diet?"

It really pisses me off to know that she has heard it all before so I tell her to leave me alone, while deciding in my head to show her this time. I really mean to succeed with this diet.

That's a massive statement because I can't stop thinking of food all day long. It's all there in the restaurant, the smell of fresh baked bread, the aroma of chicken sizzling away in the combi oven and bacon frying on the range. A heroin addict who was going cold turkey and then given a full syringe would have the same kind of tempting that I'm about to have. There are all sorts of foods lying around which I

90

should taste as a chef to make sure they are right and it will kill me not to try them.

At fifteen I was naturally thin but my mate was fourteen stone and all I wanted to do was to be the same weight as him. The trouble was when I got there, I felt too fat and it spiralled upwards to 15, 16 and 17 stone and now I am 18 stone heavy.

For twenty-five years I have been a member of a local gym and I train at least three times a week but if the truth be known, it just camouflages the flab.

Evelyn is Linda's mam and she is a lovely woman who works out and trains more than I do and she's eighty-four-years-old. Every time I see her it embarrasses me, knowing how much effort she puts in. She's a kind and thoughtful person who has worked with us in the catering business many times in the past and she was totally reliable in everything she did. We have a lot to thank her for and she is there anytime you need her, whether it's 2 o'clock in the afternoon or 2 o'clock in the morning, she will drop everything to help you. That's a rare thing in a mother-in-aw. All that and I never mentioned the carrot sandwich, Evelyn.

Evelyn's husband, Ronny, worked in the lead works for many years and lost the hearing in one ear through his job. He is a very private man who likes to keep chickens and roosters, it's something he has always done and he loves it. Perhaps Ronny's best attribute is his capacity to listen. If you need an ear to bend then Ronny is your man. I was astonished when I first met him, he used to cycle from Newcastle to the Lake District in one day but that would suit him down to the ground, just being on his own with his thoughts, It's a hell of a feat though. He always used to say to me that I was putting on weight, even when I was losing a bit.

I try and laugh off my concern by saying that I've gone up a waist size for every decade since birth but I know I'm just trying to hide my embarrassment about it.

Once, when I was shopping for a pair of jeans, the lad serving asked me what type of jeans I wanted and I said Levi 501s so he asked me what waist size and I told him 42. He just laughed and told me he was sorry but they only made them for human beings.

At that moment I should have realised that I had a big weight problem. I laughed with him but I wish the ground had opened up and swallowed me, I was so ashamed. My biggest problem is that I just blow up like a balloon. The moment I eat something, you can virtually see my body mass rising. I have a terrible fridge habit and you can find me looking in there for fifteen minutes the moment I get home, which doesn't help with weight loss one bit.

Different people have different metabolisms I know but I can go out for a few pints with my best mate and the next day, I will be half a stone heavier and he will be exactly the same as he was. It's just not fair. I've tried every diet in the world to try and lose it but none of them have really worked and today I just feel that my will power has been drained out of me.

Dieting is a mental strength thing and maybe I have none left. I have so much sympathy for all of you out there trying to lose weight. Over the years I've tried slimming tablets, water tablets, which made me collapse in the kitchen, and hypnotherapy and none of it worked.

Twenty years ago, I stopped smoking, which seemed to be

the time when all of my weight problems started. I'm not making excuses because I know that if you want to do it, you will. That's what I mean about my mental strength not being as strong as it used to be. As someone who works with food, I really should know better.

In this day and age we are bombarded with information about eating the right foods like cereal for breakfast and tuna salad or chicken and vegetables for a main meal, but putting it into practice is so difficult. I give lectures to young kids and their parents and I always tell them, don't eat badly or you'll look like me.

When I came out of Hell's Kitchen everyone told me I was a celebrity and all I could think of was, I hope they ask me into the Celebrity Fit Club programme. Stress is the killer reason I eat and I'm sure that's the same for 90% of you out there reading this.

As soon as the pressure is on, I binge on the wrong foods, never seeming to be full. There seems to be a switch in my mind which flips the moment I am under strain, it forces me to eat even though I know from the first second that it's wrong.

The car accident to Julie was a typical example. We had to travel to the hospital in Yorkshire and before we set off I raided the fridge and constantly ate for the whole journey.

As a kid I was always told to leave the table before I was full but I don't and ten minutes later, I could eat again. I lose my temper with myself but it's no good, I just have to hit the fridge. When I've stuffed myself I feel comfortable so it has to be comfort and stress eating.

Through my job in the restaurant I work unsocial hours, my body clock can go haywire and I reach for food as a distraction or a support. What really annoys me is that I am a mature forty-eight-year-old man who can't control his desire for food.

At my age I should be able to take my life in my own hands and manage my eating habits but the bad foods always win. The sugary and fatty foods always taste so wonderful that I have to have them and that's where food manufacturers know they've got you. They will never give up making and promoting these things because they make masses of money out of them.

On holiday I don't eat a quarter of the amount I eat at home. It's probably because I am in a relaxed situation. I really hope you don't think I'm going on about diets too much but I can see massive problems for everyone if things go on as they are, particularly for this generation's kids.

A good illustration about how these bad foods can capture you is me at work. There I am surrounded by the most wonderful food where I can have a fillet steak with onion rings, pepper or a diane sauce, a lobster thermadore or some good fish and what do I do? I go for a cheese sandwich, couple of pints, a bar of chocolate or an ice cream, which I tell myself I must have to cool myself down. The trouble is, when you have prepped and cooked quality food you just can't face eating it. I'm sure there are a lot of ladies out there who will relate to that.

Looking back over the years, some foods have become very controversial. eggs and salmonella started it all off. A couple of my friends were poisoned with bad eggs and to this day, they are in a very poor state of health. Eggs are a passion of mine too, I love them, but I always make sure I buy the best quality I can find. From a dietary point of view, it's important to remember that you shouldn't eat too many eggs in a week.

I have no doubt that my battle with weight will continue to the day I die and many of you will be the same. The issue of obesity in this country must be addressed now or many young people are going to die just that, young.

CHAPTER TWELVE

STAFF

In the pub trade, staff can cause a lot of problems for you. I don't know whether it's the type of business it is but you tend to get a lot of people who want to make a fast buck. Over the years we employed our fair share of them. They would dip into the till or have scams running which cost you money, so the turnover of staff is very high. Linda has always run the administration side of whichever business we have operated and I remember one year she prepared one hundred and five, P45's for staff.

It doesn't seem to matter who it is, from the chef to the cleaner, they are usually all in it.

Even the biggest chefs aren't immune. I once worked with a well-known chef from the North East who was so far up his own backside, it really pissed me off. He constantly told himself and everybody else how great he was, so his popularity was shit in the kitchen. His looking for praise never stopped but when anyone gave it to him, he would just give a snidey laugh in their direction.

It was probably the time that Linda bollocked him and he asked "Do you know who I am?" which sealed his fate. Needless to say another P45 hit the desk and he could take his fame elsewhere.

I employed a chef later on who had worked with Ego and he told me his interview had been interesting. The bloke went on and on about his own achievements, not bothering to ask what this lad had done and that sounds about right for him. As far as I'm concerned, just because one person can cook better than another, big deal. Heart is the name of the game in our business.

When you interview staff in the restaurant game you can get anyone applying from plonkys to drug addicts, which means you have to be so careful who you employ, but one thing I have noticed is that the big hitters are not necessarily the best people to use. Their egos get in the way and they can disrupt a kitchen as much as aid one, so I prefer to bring in untrained people and teach them my ways. It seems quicker in the long term to do that.

We used to have a chef whose nickname was Two Shits. Basically, anything you had done, he had gone one better. It caused no end of problems between staff, they couldn't stand him and his constant one upmanship.

Attitude goes a long way with me. If there is anything which bugs me, it's a chef whose head is too big for his hat.

Good or bad, everyone who owns a company needs staff, I just wonder why the catering industry seems to get a lot of dropouts, druggies and alcoholics. The good employees are good, the bad are total nightmares. On several occasions the bad staff try and hold you over a barrel but I won't have any of it and tell them straight to get out. I'd prefer to do their job myself as well as my own. I've always used this zero tolerance approach and it's served me well.

At the time of my wedding to Linda, we were opening a pub and had just taken on a Michelin star qualified chef. The main reception was booked at a very well-known hotel in the area and it cost an absolute fortune. Following the wedding reception at the hotel, we decided to have a buffet at my mother-in-law's house for the evening guests which would be prepared by my new chef.

I was disappointed at the basic food which was served at the hotel. It was adequate but not exactly exciting and the food apart, we had a terrific day. Your wedding day should be the best time of your life and mine was, so I didn't complain about the fare on offer.

What a contrast there was at Linda's mother's home. The buffet our new chef had created was unbelievable and it rekindled my desire to start cooking again. Oysters with bacon and Pernod, whole pineapples hollowed and filled with cream, lobsters and the largest mussels I have ever seen, competed for the guests' attention. The smells and tastes were phenomenal, it really was a banquet fit for royalty. Judging by the difference in quality and presentation of food, we should have had the entire reception at the house throughout the day.

The guy who prepared that buffet was a truly gifted chef but one evening a stranger came into the restaurant and poached his undoubted talents for his restaurant in Barbados. He has been there for twenty years then and given the choice of Stamfordham in Northumberland or a tropical paradise, I don't think he took long to make up his mind where to continue his career.

He went the way of a lot of gifted people in our industry. You can train good people to a high standard and they will be poached abroad or start their own restaurant, it's frustrating but there it is. Everybody wants to better themselves and I would be the last to stand in anyone's way if they were offered the chance of a lifetime.

My personal aim is to take young lads or girls and train them up to my standards and my ways. Good chefs will always be needed in society but the most talented and innovative are rich pickings for upmarket establishments in Dubai or some other faraway, exotic place. It's a crying shame our country loses that level of chef but you can't blame them for going. A hefty amount of my employees have moved on to very good positions, like head chef, bar manager, executive chefs or sales reps, and I wish them all well.

In a business like ours, where males and females work together over long and unsocial hours, romance rears its head often. One of the funniest things is my chefs when I employ a really attractive waitress; they become the 007 of the kitchen, their voices change and suddenly Mr Grumpy becomes the nicest man you've ever seen. The funniest thing is that they don't realise they have changed.

Sex always rears its head. I've caught so many of them getting it on and in some of the most bizarre places, like the time I caught a waiter with the lady chef de parti. They were under some stairs in the restaurant but I didn't have the heart to bollock them. Today I would have pulled them up about it, but in those days I just took the view it was natural.

It can get out of hand sometimes and then you have to put your foot down. We once had a veg store where we kept food for the kitchen. I noticed one of the dishwashing girls taking every opportunity to visit the store and she would be followed out by one of the commis, two or three minutes later.

I may not be the sharpest tool in the box but after half a dozen times, it suddenly clicked what was going on. We had a back way to the store, so I took the path and looked through the window only to see the girl on her knees in front of the chef.

I'm no prude but this kind of behaviour really got to me and I screamed at them, at which point the young lad pulled up his trousers and tidied himself. She was mortified so the strip I tore off them wasn't really necessary judging by the redness of their faces. They could do what they wanted, I told them, but not in my time. This girl caused me grief later in her career when her father called me to lay down the law, telling me how great she was. It took a massive effort not to tell him what I'd seen.

Staff can always give you a laugh and we need that in our highly pressured business. I once employed a particularly ugly lad who told me that he would be in a certain girl's knickers that was attending Christmas party. He looked like a cross between Quasimodo and King Kong so I told him he would never have a chance with such a gorgeous woman. It didn't phase him and he told me to be at the back bar window in five minutes.

It's a good job I didn't have a bet with him about it because there he was doing what comes naturally and he even turned to me, smiled and gave me a thumbs up.

In normal circumstances I would never have been so irresponsible but it being Christmas I had partaken of a few pints after service.

You always get caught when you do these things and I knew I had been, the moment the stiletto heel connected with the back of my head. Linda had seen me sneak out of the restaurant and followed me, it took some making up I can tell you.

The festive season is a typical period for losing permanent staff. At interview I always make the point that they might have to work both Christmas Day and New Year's Eve and they always assure me that it isn't a problem. When the time comes, things change. They will pack in their jobs for one day, which leaves you stranded with the busiest time of the year on your hands.

Temporary staff are even worse, they will work right up to Christmas Eve and are never seen again. It's amazing that they never come in to collect their own wages but send a friend to pick them up. They know you will lose your temper so they steer clear of the confrontation.

I was threatened with violence on one occasion. At the time, I was employing a chef who was a really good addition to the kitchen. He came to me two days before Christmas to tell me he had changed his mind and he was having Christmas Day off, despite the fact that he'd promised to work it.

There were one hundred and twenty diners expected on the day, so there was no chance of replacing him at that late stage and I told him if he didn't work the day then he needn't come back. As I squared up to him, he thought better of it. When I told him that, he just shrugged his shoulders and left, I never saw him again.

I've always tried to be fair to staff. Two of my chefs came and asked me if they could leave early one Christmas Eve to go to a party, they told me they were prepped for the next morning and would come in half an hour early to finish off so I let them go. I must have taken leave of my senses when I said yes, I even told them to have a good night, that they deserved it.

At 9am the next morning, I arrived to get ready for service at noon. To say I was under pressure would be an understatement. Running around like a headless chicken, I waited for them to come in and as 10am passed there was no sign of either of them. The longer the time went on, I became more and more stressed out, calling them all sorts of names under my breath.

Radio One was blaring out Christmas carols and I felt about as festive as a grumpy Scrooge. My feelings of disappointment were massive. At 11.30 I knew I was fighting a losing battle and called both Linda and one of the waiters into the kitchen to help out.

The food for a Christmas Day is varied so I just tried to get on preparing for service by readying the turkey, duck with rich orange gravy and salmon with hollandaise. I'd sorted the veg into terrines so the waiters could put it in the steamers and get the food away, it couldn't have been any more manic than Fawlty Towers.

One of the chefs rolled in casually at 11.45am to say he was sorry. In my madness, I couldn't speak to him and gave him a look which showed my displeasure in no uncertain fashion.

An hour later, the other chef pitched up and he was still pissed. I could have cheerfully killed him but I just told him to get away from the place. As he left he turned and told me to stick my job up my arse. The other one started to put his opinions into the conversation so I asked him if he was proud of himself. At that point he joined his friend and left. They were two real scumbags of the industry.

I've never seen either of them to this day but I've heard they are both head chefs now and I only hope they have the same treatment at Christmas that they gave me.

There's no doubt that alcohol rules some people who work in the catering industry. The environment of hard work, heat and stress turns peoples' minds to it. I've been forced to intervene often when employees have taken things too far.

Split shifts are the problem along with the changes in licensing laws, staff will leave the kitchen at 3pm for a two hour break and rather than go home, will spend the time in the pub.

In my establishments they are well warned in advance that excessive drinking can't be allowed over that period. When they return from a split, I watch them very carefully and if they are going to be a danger to themselves or others, or can't perform to the best of their ability, they are sent home.

Drugs are not tolerated under any circumstances. I've seen people arrive at work with eyes like Uncle Festa's, they think you can't tell what they have been up to but I can spot the glazed look a mile away.

Don't believe for a second that I don't drink myself, I do but it's always well after service is complete and the kitchen is cleaned down. I like drink as much as the next man but it has to be at the right time and in the right place.

In my time as a chef, I have seen people who have operated kitchen machinery and used knives that would be three or more times over the legal limit for driving. What's more frightening are the bosses who allow this behaviour to go on and, in some cases, encourage it.

My attitude to all this comes from a time when I stayed up one night to watch an important Frank Bruno fight with one of my bar managers. Spirits were the order of the night and he encouraged me to join him in a competition to have a shot from every optic.

It was 4am before I got to bed. That wouldn't have been so bad but I didn't leave it for three days. Anyone who has had a good session knows the feelings that come along with recovery - hot and cold sweats, retching sickness and the regular bouts of wanting death to come along.

The bar manager was back to work at 10am the next morning, feeling on top of the world and I looked like an unhealthy corpse. Linda waited until I recovered then told me that if it happened ever again she would be off. We all need a good woman to bring us back from the brink sometimes. From that moment in time I have avoided any session of that magnitude.

I employed a pastry chef on the recommendation of this particular bar manager. Wherever he worked, the chefs would follow him, he was that popular in the industry.

The pastry chef was an outstanding worker and really talented but she had another talent which I discovered some time later. If there was trouble in the pub, she would act like an extra bouncer, pitching in with her rolling pin to sort out the hardest of troublemakers, wading in like Wonder Woman.

The moment I get an inkling that a chef is going to cause trouble, I know it's time to be rid of him. Most chefs have an ego, it comes with the territory but some can be a real problem.

There was one lad I employed who I knew socially but I still gave him a job, knowing there could be problems along the way. In fairness to him, he was a good lad but he just courted trouble and found it wherever he turned. It's not an ideal situation to work with someone you know outside of work, they tend to try and take advantage of the friendship, so I try and avoid it these days.

One of my real pet hates is a chef who wears a bandana. This one turned up on the first day wearing one so it was a bit of a bad start. He looked like an extra from Pirates of the Caribbean, all he needed was a cutlass to finish off the picture.

I'm not a chef who has strict rules about hats, so long as their hair is short. What I really can't stand is a dirty chef's uniform which hasn't seen an iron in months. The chef I am talking about didn't have any problems in that direction, but he was a bit of a wimp where pain was concerned.

In a kitchen it's inevitable that you will get burns or cuts and you get used to them, this one had cut his finger and the fuss he made about it was incredible. I really can't stand trivialities so if a chef comes to me with a cut I don't even look at it, all I'm concerned about is the fact they keep blood away from the food. I am obsessive about cleanliness and hygiene so I always make sure anyone's cuts are covered securely. In this day and age you have to be very cautious where those things are concerned.

Actually, the cut was very bad on this occasion, so my disregard of the situation wasn't justified. The moment I saw it, I sent him to hospital. It made me one team hand down but

I knew I was right to do it.

When I saw him the following day he was a bit pale and told me he had to have an operation on the wound later that afternoon. He would also be away from work for six weeks, that was a blow for me.

Of course his health came first, but when I found out the cause of the cut, I went ballistic. I asked him how it had happened and he came out with a believable story, but a pack of lies. Witnesses in the kitchen told me he had been tossing a knife in the air and catching it to impress the female staff. As always happens when you prat about in the kitchen, it comes back to bite you in the arse and, inevitably, he caught the blade instead of the handle.

The six weeks passed and he returned to work, only to slip and put his hand in the fat fryer. It was obvious he wasn't going to find catering his best line of work so I asked him to leave of his own accord. I think he knew I was right and we shook hands and kept our friendship.

Burns can be a major problem, you can spend time on small burns but the big ones need a lot more attention than you can give at the restaurant. Over an average week, I will have a couple of serious blisters but I just get on with the work and any chef will tell you that you just have to soldier on. It becomes nondescript after a while.

Most staff in the catering industry are obliging in their outlook to work and will turn their hands to different things if asked, going well beyond the call of duty.

My chefs have cut grass, painted, tiled, dressed up as Santa Claus and even waited on tables when I've asked them to if the front of house staff are short. I can't think of another profession where staff would change hats like that and help out to that extent so I really feel they are special people.

In my years as a chef I have performed every job from the lowest to the highest, so I'm not asking someone to do anything I haven't done myself, including cleaning the loos. Still today, I get every new member of staff to clean the toilets and they look at me in disbelief when I tell them to do it. The fact is that they also crap and piss in it so they can have a go at cleaning it as well.

I once had a young lad who was a doctor's son while he was at university in the city and, for about a year, he peeled veg for me. For a long time he was preparing sprouts, peeling the outer layer and putting the cross in the in the bottom. He asked if he could do them at home so I gave him some bags and told him I'd pay him a fiver a bag. He took six full ones away. The following day he turned up with them completed, telling me his parents and brothers had helped him while they watched television. His father was a G.P. so it just goes to show that parents will do anything to help their kids. Every time I went to see the doctor after that, I would have a bit of a giggle to myself.

The catering industry isn't the best paid profession in the world so I'm often asked for a sub from the staff, sometimes the day after they've been paid. I am a real sucker for a sob story so when I'm told the wife needs to buy school uniform or the building society is going to repossess the house, it tugs at my heart strings.

One bloke who worked with me for six years was in a lot of trouble with a money lender and owed him £600 so I loaned him the amount, on the understanding I would take £50 a week from his wages. You've probably guessed it but after a couple of weeks I never saw him again. Sadly, I thought he was a friend as well as employee and that kind of thing makes it harder for the next guy coming in.

I think the bloke's conscience must have pricked him because he moved away from the area and told me he would send me the outstanding money when he got it. Yet again I believed him and yet again Linda told me how soft I was. Maybe one day I'll learn the lesson.

I've already mentioned cleanliness. In my view the most important hygiene requirement in a kitchen is personal attention. Well groomed hair, clean skin, being clean shaven, along with a smart appearance goes a long way to making a kitchen the cleanest environment possible.

Whenever I interview someone for a job, I take a very good look at them, some of them smell like Ghandi's flip flops and how they can let themselves smell and look the way they do is beyond me. Remember, we are talking food here.

From a general standpoint, I'll drum into my staff to be courteous, treat their jobs like an athlete, be fit and ready and to check any deliveries coming into the restaurant.

Suppliers can cause problems for a restaurant by delivering goods which are damaged or unchecked. That kind of thing can easily be slipped through by a supplier, so my staff are instructed to check deliveries fully before accepting them.

You can't just change supplier to ensure the best; I've tried the smallest to the biggest and they will all try to slip by things which are coming up to use by dates. Food has even been sent to me with one day left on the use by and that's no damned good to a restaurant. My staff are told to check everything the moment it arrives.

I'm forty seven now so I tell the youngsters that it isn't

about me anymore. It's about them going on and making a name for themselves in the industry. I try as much as possible to get a healthy competition going between them, to engender some pride in what they do and most of the time it works.

At the moment, Paul is the souffle king, Roger the tatin king, Shane the pomme anne king and Danny the chip king, and they're all proud of the fact they have a role to play in the success of the restaurant.

Danny is a lad fresh out of prison. He came to see me when I was setting up my new restaurant, to ask for a job. His honesty impressed me so I took him on and now he is holding his own. I've told him, if he cocks it up he isn't letting anyone down but himself and I don't think he will let it slip.

So that's my outlook on staff. Your business is only as good as the people you employ and I have been very lucky by and large with the people I've engaged.

CHAPTER THIRTEEN

TURNING THE CORNER

In our business stress is a major factor. Linda and I have had a lot of highs, lows, arguments and unhappiness to contend with. A lot of that came from running past restaurants, when we seemed to be constantly in the red.

Like most other business people, no matter how much money we took in, it seemed to be going out just as quickly or even faster. That's a recipe for disaster where personal relationships are concerned.

Linda has always handled the monetary side of our ventures and she used to juggle the cash from our personal account to the business one to keep us afloat. Times were really hard, our rent was very high in our establishments at £1200 a week, the rates were £12,000 per year and the gas and electric bills were phenomenal. All this was required before we bought any food or paid any wages so it was crippling.

We needed some other source of income and I was lucky to be able to use the personal mortgage when living in the pub to finance the renovation of odd flats.

It started with a couple of run down properties which I managed to do up and sell and we continued by buying a house in a place called Dissington. I used to handle the refurbishments through the day and then work in the kitchen at night. It almost killed me and I'll never know how my body and brain coped.

At the time, Linda and I were doing a bit of outside catering but it didn't help, we never seemed to get on top of the outgoings. We were as much as £10,000 overdrawn and it was starting to climb frighteningly but luckily the house was finished at about this time and we sold it for a substantial sum. You've no idea how that took the pressure off us as a couple and we thought great, we're back on top, we should have realised that it wasn't going to last long.

One evening, a bloke came into the restaurant to eat and told me the meal was fantastic, he asked to see me and wanted to know if I was capable of cooking for 300-400 people.

It turned out he was one of the directors of a very large local brewery which has a massive function suite. All sorts of major functions went on there, from sportsman's dinners to upmarket weddings and important award ceremonies.

Now, I am a cautious person and thought, shit this is massive but Linda is never phased and just told him it was no problem. I could have killed her at that moment. From then on we agreed a saying we have always stuck to and that is, take the job, no matter how big and worry about it later, and then we laugh the manic laugh.

That's been our motto for the last ten years and it hasn't let us down. Mind you, the first attempt was a bit of a disaster, or at least that's how I saw it.

Our initial job for the brewery was a function for three hundred and fifty. They wanted a three course meal and when we got to the venue, it became obvious we had a problem with the hired equipment. The old saying is 'a good workman shouldn't blame his tools', but more often than not it's the supply of unknown and untested gear which lets you down.

I decided to try and plate the meals straight from the ovens but trying to plate up five to six items for three to four hundred people was a recipe for disaster. We managed to serve everyone a hot meal but it was so slow. As I looked at the lady banqueting manageress, her expression said it all, no words were needed. She just scowled at me from a distance. I knew exactly how she felt.

Be thankful you haven't heard me when something goes wrong like that, I rant and rave because it's not something I can control. My reaction to things like that is better than a fire for clearing an area, they scatter like frightened rabbits as soon as they see things going wrong.

There were a few other companies in for the job and the brewery was going to pick the best of the bunch. One company ran out of food and were unable to feed a few full tables then scarpered out the door in shame, when they realised what they'd done.

Another company forgot to switch on the hot cupboards and couldn't serve the meal required so they were quickly dropped and we were picked as the best of the available caterers which was a surprise, considering we hadn't done a great job.

The next time I came across the lady manageress she told

me that we hadn't been too bad and if that was the case, heaven knows how bad the others had been.

To make sure we sorted out the equipment situation, we decided to buy our own hot cupboards and chose a good quality, expensive type. We didn't want to be caught out in any aspect of the potential functions and purchased a thousand-piece dinner service and cutlery. The money we had made on the sale of the house we had renovated was taken up with these purchases but the peace of mind it gave us was phenomenal.

One of the things that worried us at the time was the brewery didn't give us a contract, so the risk to us was enormous, but you need to speculate to accumulate sometimes and this was one of them.

Working under those pressures piles massive amounts of stress on your shoulders. You're only as good as your last meal and I knew if I cocked up, we would be in deep, deep shit.

That first December when we started cooking for the brewery functions, we were also toiling flat out in the pub restaurant and we were often exhausted to the point of collapse.

It was a particularly busy time at the suite in the run up to Christmas with 14,000 diners booking for the festive meals. The preparation was immense and two of the guys I had employed were doing eighty hours a week just slicing turkey. They told me afterwards they never wanted to see another bloody turkey as long as they lived and I couldn't blame them.

I bought in the veg ready prepped, which made things easier all round. Buying veg ready prepared is hugely expensive but there is a massive saving in labour cost so you don't lose much at the end of the day. When you are dealing with the numbers we cater for, any labour saving scheme is a big help to the bottom line.

That Christmas was one of the best we ever had and most people went home happy with a good impression of the function suite. In fact, we only had two complaints out of 14,000 servings and the banquet manageress was ecstatic. She told us that on previous Januarys, she had to spend almost all her time dealing with dissatisfied customers so we had made her job that much easier.

At the same time we were providing outside catering services we were continuing with the pub food and making a huge success of that side too. The bank manager loved us, we were slowly but surely getting back on a solid footing in banking terms. Linda and I knew that the time could come around again easily when we were £40,000 in debt once more and that fact, along with the threatened robbery we had experienced, convinced us to quit the pub. It was a wrench to give it up but it didn't take a rocket scientist to decide on the best course after everything that had happened to us while in charge.

When I was working in the pub I was constantly sick of toiling in a closed kitchen with no exposure to the customers. All I ever saw were waiters and waitresses and they aren't the sunniest bunch when the pressure is on. I used to get abusive and angry to everyone in that sealed area and one day Linda stepped in and told me I needed to face the customers for a change.

I decided to take her up on the offer and changed my whites for a waiter's uniform. The first thing I noticed in the dining room was how pleasant you have to be with customers, no matter what you feel inside. I thought it was quite easy to do that until I got into it. My first customers were a large family and the first thing ordered was three types of unusual cocktail, immediately I'm on the back foot and shouting for help as I'm panicking.

As I look around at my customers they are sitting down at their choice of tables and they begin to take chairs from other tables to sit everybody. Linda smiles and tells me to tell them not to move the furniture.

Not being the most tactful person in the world I tell them straight to leave the chairs alone. They look at me and ask what the problem is so I tell them that other customers will suffer. It's at this point they get up and tell me to stick my chairs up my arse. They begin to walk out but Linda cuts them off, telling me as she passes to get behind the bar. Within a minute she has the party laughing and settling down to order, after returning the chairs to their original places. As Linda passes me she has a massive smirk on her face.

Two days later I'm serving in the bar when two policemen enter and tell me I've been serving under age drinkers. As I look at the two lads the police have brought with them, I recognise them as two I'd served earlier and who looked well over eighteen. As I take a closer look they would be hard pressed to pass for twelve.

It's my turn to smirk as I tell them Linda is the licensee and call her over. Luckily the lads had been eating so they were entitled to a drink but it was a close shave. She glares over to some people who have their feet on her new coffee table, telling me to sort it out and I'm on my way over when a bloke stops me and shouts that his food is shit, the veg is supposedly cold and the sauce is lumpy. His wife's food didn't arrive until ten minutes after his and he's not a happy bunny.

This is a little bit more important than the coffee table offenders so I take his food away and offer him a free drink as he tells me that all he wants is a decent meal. Once in the kitchen, I go ballistic with the chef's. Our new head chef told me at interview that he was the greatest thing since sliced bread but as I look at the check board, I can see he isn't handling it very well. It's now I tell him to get his fucking act together, get the two meals out and they better be perfect.

A couple of other incidents happen while I am in my waiting mode and by the time close of service comes I tell Linda she's won and the waiting game is definitely not for me.

It was time to start Miller Catering, our outdoor catering business, but there was the little matter of giving the landlord of the pub our notice of quitting and his reaction wasn't the most pleasant as he began to call us some very choice names, while threatening us with solicitors' letters and anything else legal he could think of.

I can't describe the feeling of relief I had when walking away from that business, it was like a ton weight had been lifted from my shoulders, without doubt it was the second best day of my life.

We had hired a unit just prior to leaving the pub and we started Miller Catering the moment we left the restaurant. Our reputation had begun to be realised so new customers were coming to us almost daily for Millers' services. The money was still hard to come by, giving us no option but to work every hour God sent. No job was too small for Linda and me, from dishwashing to emptying bins.

Over the years, we've worked with many celebrities, some of them good and some of them egotistical to the point they almost thought they were God. In fairness, most of them were nice people like George Best and Ken Dodd.

Doddy asked me for a spare meal at one function, saying, "The size of you, it's a wonder there's anything left for anyone else". Everyone else says he's tight but he slipped me a fiver so he definitely wasn't miserly with me.

The pride I felt at cooking for the likes of Dennis Law, Gazza and my hero Shearer, when they attended these functions was indescribable, and I just lapped up the sportsman's dinners and entertainment functions we were involved with.

When everything goes right and four or five hundred people ask to see the chef, the buzz can't be beaten by anything else. The compliments fly but I always tell my lads to remember that compliments don't buy drinks.

A million and one things go wrong when you are catering for large parties, like the time I had to think fast on my feet and turn vegetable soup into carrot and coriander by lacing it with tumeric at the last minute. That's when a chef's improvisation comes into play.

I've seen Linda go on stage in front of hundreds of diners to say, "If your apple pie tastes like cheesecake that's because it is, it's the printers' fault". She gets a laugh when she does that kind of thing but before she tells them, I am a nervous wreck.

Sometimes I feel I should be split into a thousand parts, we have that many functions going at once. There have been days when we've catered for one thousand dinners but they've been split into separate rooms of two hundred and fifty in one room, six hundred in another, two hundred in another and so on.

Imagine the temps I have to draft in along with agency staff, family and anyone else I can get my hands on. I've even had Sales Reps helping me, telling them that if they do, I will buy my supplies from them, that's the kind of things you have to do to get the job done.

Sometimes I will ask an agency for chefs and waitresses and I'll ask the chefs how long they have been qualified so that I can get a feel of what they are capable of. Most of them have a couldn't care less attitude and they tell me they have only started with the agency that day which is more than hard to believe.

Usually they will turn out to be one of the chefs' brothers who has been drafted in and, because the agency has no time left to get anyone else on the day, I have to give them menial jobs to do.

At the function suite we used to cook on the ground floor, sending the meals to the various rooms on the first and second, an added complication was that we couldn't use the lifts. I can say now that we broke every rule in the book to get the job done in transporting those plates.

With sixty to seventy waiting staff on duty, the arguments were uncontrollable and I've had to wade in to stop several fights over the years. The boys can be bad but the girls can hold their own believe me.

One girl had a drink problem and always seemed pissed but I could never pin anything on her until I found her pop bottle filled with vodka secreted behind the loo.

Thankfully, we started to benefit financially from all the hard work and money was starting to find a permanent home in the bank, it got to the extent where our business was getting bigger by the day.

Things were finally starting to look up when BANG, the brewery was sold to another company and for no reason we were given the chop. I began to wonder if there was a God and if there was, what particular wrong I had done to him and then he gave me something which sweetened the blow in the form of Hell's Kitchen. He always seems to look after me when the chips are down.

After the show finished, my main priority was opening the restaurant and a new company won the tender for the brewery business.

YOU NEVER KNOW WHAT'S AROUND THE CORNER.

CHAPTER FOURTEEN

THE GREAT OUTDOORS

C ooking in a restaurant is one thing, cooking for an outside event is quite another. There isn't much I don't know about the outdoor catering industry. I've prepared and made food for functions in marquees, caravans, barns, houses, offices, you name it and I've done it.

I've barbecued for kids, adults, women's parties and any other gathering you can name and sometimes I wish I'd barbecued the kids instead of barbecuing the food.

If you'll pardon the expression, balls are straightforward affairs for me, the trouble is that the organisers see it appears an easy thing to do and they decide the following year to give it a bash themselves. It's like me putting on Shearer's boots and turning out against Manchester United, it doesn't work.

They wonder why it's a flop and if I thought I could beat Rio Ferdinand just because I was wearing the great man's boots, I'd be a flop too. We're constantly told of the fiascos by guests who have attended these do it yourself catering attempts.

The only problems we have at these functions is when the organiser sub contracts us to do the party and we charge £10 - £12 per head for a three or four course meal and they charge their tickets at £40 per head.

It's phenomenal the number of times we are told the meal isn't worth the money and of course it isn't but our hands are tied and we aren't allowed to comment.

Outside catering is a nightmare in the winter. On Valentine's Day one year, we had a job booked in a marquee in the middle of Northumberland. The day was sunny but freezing cold and the job in hand was a ball but the Army base it was taking place at, was forty-five miles away so we needed to get as much equipment there as possible.

As soon as we arrived we knew that the day was a potential disaster, it was at least minus ten and there were four hundred and fifty to feed. We offloaded the vehicle of ovens, fryers, urns, tables etc and my hands were blue from touching the chilling metal. To top it all off, I had forgotten my top coat and Mr Grumpy came into play.

Whenever you do these events you have to locate the power source first but there was no permanent power sockets, they were using a generator. The trouble is that they are normally sited well away from the marquee because of the noise they make. You've probably guessed it but my extension leads weren't long enough. I am reluctant to ask organisers for help more than a couple of times or they lose confidence in you so I looked at my watch and started to panic. If I sent the van back for longer leads it would take about two hours which I didn't have, but there was no choice and the moment the vehicle was unloaded it was sent back for them.

My foul mood started, where I was raving and shouting at everyone in sight to get the food up. The lads plated it and it would be regened later, just before service. The day had got off to a bad start and it would get worse, I just knew.

My next job was to find a water source to cook the massive amount of vegetables for that amount of people and to get the coffee started and thaw everyone out. The hose was just about long enough to reach the tap, trouble was that no water was coming out of the thing, it was frozen solid. Our organiser's face showed his contempt when I asked for help and he made me feel like something on the bottom of his shoe, the look on his face told me I had overstepped the mark.

Eventually, we got the water back to the marquee in pans but it had already iced up and that day was the longest time it has ever taken me to cook veg. The damned water just wouldn't come to the boil and the words al dente came to mind.

Our spirits rose when the van returned with the leads, everything was finally coming together I thought, until I looked at the sockets and they were a caravan type and ours weren't. Another two hours back to base for some more or should I risk asking the organiser for more help? Because of the journey times back and forth there wasn't really a choice.

Time was moving on, it was 4pm, the organiser is pissed off with me and I was asking for more aid. They had none of the right sort at the location but he reluctantly told me he might be able to borrow some leads from the local garage.

When he got back, he literally threw them on the floor at my feet and I felt like a piece of shit. Normally I would have said something to him but on this occasion I didn't have

Linda with me and I just wanted to get on with the job and get out of there.

Twice during the day, the electric tripped so when the evening began we were all keeping our fingers crossed. It had only been off for a couple of minutes but it would have been disastrous for us if it happened again.

The band plugged in and the bar was beginning to operate when everything was plunged into darkness. It had happened again and it was my turn to gloat because this was the organiser's baby and the buck passed to him. I put in some little snidey comments, just to let him know what it was like to be on the other side of the fence which he didn't like at all.

He was absolutely foaming when I smiled and told him I couldn't cook without electricity and he would have to do something about it. It was time to keep him on the ropes when he asked if we could help him, the trip switch was in the kitchen area of the marquee. Could we cook in the dark he wanted to know? My hesitation for the few seconds until he was forced to say please was really satisfying, I wanted him to squirm as much as possible. I thought back over his attitude to me through the day and realised we were quits now.

The cooking process through the night was interesting, cooking by the glow of the gas rings we couldn't see how much sauce to put on the meals, or how much cream was needed in the sweet.

Our efforts seemed in vain when a massive food fight started between the diners. There was food everywhere, covering everything. People were slipping on cream, their clothes saturated with sauce. It was like something out of the

Wild West.

Whenever there is a food fight, the reason is usually that the food is crap, so now I was worried that we wouldn't be paid after the horrendous day we'd had.

At the end of it all we started to clear up the mess. God alone knows how long it took but we managed it eventually.

I was curious about the food fight and the reason it happened but when I asked him about it, he told me not to worry about that, It hadn't been the quality of the food at all and I went away finally happy.

The organiser's attitude had changed completely at the end of the service, telling me that he was delighted with our work. As he handed me the cheque he said, see you next year, the food fight happens EVERY year.

One show we catered for was the largest in the North East and they were expecting 20,000 people, which is serious numbers.

Imagine the amount of things going through your head when trying to work out what you will need. How many hot dogs, buns, chips, beef dinners or vegetarians will there be? It's a bloody nightmare.

There were judges, contestants, workers, all needing to be fed and all in different areas. It was a massive logistical exercise. The cold rooms were loaded up with stock and I pleaded with my main supplier for the mountain of food I needed. It was funny watching a freezer artic wagon staggering onto the site.

It was a weekend do with an early start of 5am the first day. Glancing across the site, I saw the largest marquee I have ever seen, it was the size of a football pitch. By 7am the stress was already building to pressure cooker proportions, with staff needing fed first and early. As stress goes, that weekend would have been hard to beat and it also turned out to be the hottest day of the entire year.

As soon as we arrived at the site, I approached the organisers to find out where the water was located and they marched me about a thousand metres across a field to a standpipe. It was time to put my thinking cap on. The only way we could get water to the marquee was via hosepipes and we spent ages joining a large number of them together.

As soon as we had done this, Environmental Health turned up, flashing their badges and told us that the pipes needed to be sterilised. I sent one of the staff to a store for some Milton sterilising solution and we blasted it through the pipes and then flushed them through with water.

People came to us all day complaining that their tea and coffee had a hint of bleach to it but there was nothing we could do about it. No matter how many flushes we did, we couldn't get rid of the residue. At least Environmental Health were happy but I was worried that the food cooked in water would have the same hint of the solution taste.

In the end, the complaints were so numerous that I had to send the van with twenty large containers to the standpipe for fresh water but driving back across a bumpy field meant that 90% of the liquid was lost. As a chef, it's not my responsibility to sort out the water situation but if I hadn't, the function could not have taken place.

The next time you are sweating, cooking a barbecue on a hot day, spare a thought for chefs who have to cook at these places for thousands in similar heat.

6pm came and there wasn't enough food left to fill an overstuffed ant. It was then I started panicking about the food required for the next day. Sundays aren't the best days to source food so I telephoned a big cash and carry called Makro. They told me they had lots of stuff, so I set off with two large hire vans and cleared the place of every ounce of food they had, there wasn't a chip, burger, sausage and beef joint left in the cash and carry.

You might think that solved the problem but then Linda, my son Anthony and myself had to return to prep the lot. I think I actually hit bed at three in the morning and at five the alarm sounded like a klaxon once again, waking us for another joyous day. Linda promptly collapsed when she got out of bed and that is the only time I have ever seen her in that state, I've never even seen her close to it. She wasn't pleased when I made her get back into bed but I told her it wasn't worth putting her life at risk for business.

As we set off, I knew in the back of my mind we couldn't cope without her and as dawn came up, I saw the weather had changed dramatically, it started to piss down and the wipers couldn't cope with the amount.

We were pulling into the show's location and, through a misted windscreen I saw Linda giving the waitresses their orders for the day. She had driven a different route to avoid seeing me because she knew I would have insisted she went home but to be honest I just smiled because I knew the day would be a success with her. I told her she was crazy but she just ignored me and got on with it like she always does.

We nearly killed ourselves getting everything ready but we needn't have bothered because hardly anyone turned up, due to the weather. Imagine the fortune we lost in food and the aftermath of cleaning went on for days.

The organisers had wanted everything for nothing and we

even had to pay them for the marquee later on, no wonder I said I never wanted to see a show again. Wor lass has a great sixth sense about people and if she gets the slightest feeling something isn't quite right, we knock the job on the head. She can spot someone who won't pay their bill a mile off and the moment she tells me she has a problem with someone we refuse the job.

In an outdoor catering business like Millers, we regularly have a number of different jobs on the same day which occasionally means I have to bring in agency staff to run those events. Linda and I will split up if there are two events so that one of us at least is there keeping an eye on what's going on.

The trouble is that we can have two or three marquee weddings, a sportsman's dinner and an interior wedding on the same day and we can't run everything personally. Christmas and mid summer periods are the worst for this. That's when you have to rely on someone else and that's when problems can occur but, thankfully for us, we haven't had many problems except on one notable occasion.

There was a venue I had been catering regularly for and one year I had another job on the same day as this event. Don't ask me why but I decided to oversee the other task and leave the longstanding event to a chef I knew to run. He'd been in the job a long time but had left the trade for a while when he asked me if I had any work, and with Christmas looming, I knew I was going to need as much help as I could lay my hands on.

I had been catering at the regular job for six years and thought this bloke would be all right to handle this important do.

As a company we had an incredible record where complaints were concerned. I could count on the fingers of one hand the number we had over many years, it was a performance that gave us a lot of pride. This one event shattered all that though, with thirty-odd criticisms about the food.

Just before the day of the event, I had gone through everything with this chef, showing him in detail how to handle the service but he wanted to do it his way. It isn't the chef who gets it in the neck but Millers Catering, that's who gets the showing up. More importantly, it's me who has to foot the bill for this type of cock up and it's a bloody expensive exercise. Linda's description of this bloke was really accurate, she just used one word, BUTCHER.

The complaints ranged from freezing food, as one punter put it, to general taste problems. On his way to the job, he hadn't tied down the equipment in the van correctly with the result that he smashed ovens, handles and plates etc. If I had got my hands on him on the day, I would cheerfully have throttled him.

I'd left him to his own devices and retained him because I needed the cover over the festive season so he went to another job where he burned the soup and then the sauce for the Christmas pudding. We had a serious problem but however much it was going to hurt us to be a man down over Christmas, this bloke had to go. Linda was adamant he wasn't doing another job for Millers so she went into her wardrobe, pulling out her kit and organised the waitresses in the afternoon and then donned her whites in the evening to take on the chef's duties.

I expected the wrath we got from the companies involved

because we had really let them down, I was just praying that this chef would be banished from the planet, the way he'd been banished from Millers.

CHAPTER FIFTEEN

CUSTOMERS

O ver the years, I have met thousands of customers and most of them are really nice people but just occasionally you get a complete arsehole. As a restaurateur, I'm not sure whether this chapter of the book will do me any favours or not but I'm going to tell you of some people and incidents over time which have caused me heartache.

There is no reason to tell you about the nice regular customers we have, that would be boring for you but the others can give everything from a serious problem to a good laugh so here goes.

One man used to be a regular diner in one of our restaurants, his wife unfortunately was wheelchair bound and was in such a state that we had to help in many ways when they came in.

Julie is a really loving person and she took on a lot of the tasks in helping this lady, including aiding her with her meal so the man could eat comfortably at the same time.

No matter how busy we were, Julie would always spend quality time with the couple. They really were a nice pair of people and we had a lot of time for them.

I was in the kitchen cooking one day when I saw them arrive and gave them a friendly wave and started to prepare this lady's meal, which would take about twenty minutes to get ready.

Suddenly Julie literally ran into the kitchen, looking flustered with her face beetroot red. She could hardly get her words out and eventually asked me what she was going to do. I took hold of her and tried to calm her down a bit, asking her to tell me what the problem was.

Apparently the man had asked to see Julie privately in the foyer. When they got there he told her how fantastic she was looking after his wife and then, out of the blue asked if she would go out on a date with him. She was twenty-eight at the time and he was in his fifties and it took her breath away when he came out with that.

It didn't stop Julie always being attentive with the woman but each time they came in, she was terrified it would all happen again. I can see why he fell for Julie, she is a beautiful girl and has a heart of gold and let's face it, most of us can't imagine the pressure looking after a disabled wife day in, day out can be.

A couple of beers after service is always a nice thing for me and it gives me the chance to meet the clientele. I keep the drinking to a minimum, it's just a social thing and I get great feedback about the food.

One night I was standing in the cocktail bar when a very beautiful and well dressed woman came up to me. She was a bit of a stunner it has to be said, she told me that the meal had been wonderful and I thanked her for her comments. We exchanged niceties but she went on and on about the quality of the meal. I was absolutely gob smacked when she said that the sticky toffee pudding was as good as an orgasm. The woman was almost on top of me by this time and Linda was standing glowering in the background. I was totally flustered and mumbled something about being pleased she enjoyed it. She said it again so I smiled and said I was pleased she'd had a good night and then she squeezed my arm saying, "That depends on who you end up in bed with".

By this time I am crapping myself. I'm usually confident around women but this vamp was seriously threatening, it was offered on a plate but in earshot of my wife, all I could think of saying was, "Linda, help". I bet you think I'm a right wimp.

One of the most unsavoury incidents is a very sad story but true story and it happened when we owned a pub restaurant some years ago. For many weeks we had been having a problem with the male toilets, the toilet floor was awash with urine and the smell was overpowering. No matter how much we tried to deal with it, the problem continued to get worse. I had to regularly strip off my chef's whites, dress in overalls and try and sort out the situation. The amount of times I had to wash myself before returning to the kitchen was incredible. Linda was going on at me every day about the state of the toilet, saying I was handy as a plumber so why couldn't I sort it. All I could think of was the cleaners causing the problem by using those blue and green toilet blocks. I was coming to the end of my tether until I found out the cause.

There was an old gentleman who was a regular in the pub and I soon discovered he was having considerable problems with his waterworks and that he was the cause of the problem because he was pissing on the toilet floor. It actually got to the stage where I had to follow him to the toilet and hold a bucket in place for him, now you can tell how glamorous the catering industry is.

He was a really canny old soul and I liked him a lot so I told him when he needed the loo he should tell me and I would help him with the bucket each time. We became very good friends; he introduced me to crackers and cheese covered in English mustard which I now love.

This bloke's wife didn't like him drinking so he developed a system for sneaking a quick drink at home. His better half didn't like Lucozade so he would fill one of their bottles with brandy and leave it in the fridge, taking a sip every now and then. She even used to tell him to have a quick swig before he went to bed and he was happy as a pig in shit.

Jack Charlton, the ex Republic of Ireland and Newcastle manager used to come to the pub and I was fortunate enough to strike up a good friendship with him. He is a keen fisherman as most people know so he promised me the first salmon he caught on the river Tyne that season and he was as good as his word, bringing in a good specimen.

I duly placed the salmon on the menu board with reference it had been caught by Jack and sat back to wait the orders for it. The trouble was that no one believed it was caught by Jack and not one portion left the kitchen.

There was also the time when we received a booking from a male customer who reserved a table for his wife and himself on the evening of the same day.

As it turned out, we had a problem with the heating and wanted to move him to a different part of the restaurant so I rang the man at home to tell him of the problem. He wasn't in so I talked to his wife and explained the situation. She told me I must be mistaken as her husband was in London on business that day.

When the evening arrived, the man turned up with a stunning woman. Call me old fashioned but I really don't think she was his wife, they were paying far too much attention to each other for a married couple. I decided to bite the bullet and tell him of my call to his wife. The man seemed to take it in his stride and assured me that it was all right. Even now I wonder how he explained this little incident when he got home. I hope it was all worth it.

The pub restaurant I'm referring to had two tiers and the upper level windows overlooked the car park. There was a married lady who was obviously not very happy at home because she had taken a lover and used to visit the pub regularly with her man on the side. She must have been a very confident person because she would come in one week with the lover and the next with her husband, it was quite bizarre.

The lads used to pile up to the windows on the nights when the lover was in play, just to see what would happen in the car outside. They used to take a sweepstake on how long the man would last and timed it all from the moment the woman's feet touched the dashboard, thirty seconds to a minute and a half was the average. Not bad going I thought!

Even the richest people aren't averse to a bit of nicking and one night the head waiter told me that two crystal glasses had gone missing from a table he had just cleared in the restaurant. The party was just in the process of leaving and he had seen the man slip one of the glasses into his pocket.

I stood in the foyer waiting for them to come out of the

dining area and as he came towards me, he congratulated me on the meal. I thanked him but asked for my glasses back, at which point he looked grieved and told me he didn't know what I was talking about in his ever so posh accent.

There was a big bulge in his pocket where the glass was so I don't know why he even tried to deny it and he realised the game was up, taking out the item he placed it on the table and left.

Next to appear was his wife, asking where her husband had gone so I told her he had just gone and had left the glass he'd stolen from me. She got really indignant saying that her husband would never do things like that, I just sighed and told her to leave the other glass she had in her handbag.

If I thought it was going to embarrass her, I was wrong. She told me not to be so stupid, that she would never do a thing like that. It was getting out of hand now and I told her she had a choice of removing it or the police being called. That was enough to make her mind up and she placed it on the table next to the other one. Amazingly, I watched them drive off in a Rolls Royce.

The stealing didn't end there, it never does actually. Two weeks later I was cutting the grass outside the pub when two paintings were lobbed out of the ladies' toilet window, landing at the bottom of the wall. As there were only two people in the restaurant, I knew they had to be the culprits so I walked over and removed the paintings and waited for them to leave.

I hid myself and watched the scene unfold. The woman walked over to the area below the window looking for her ill-gotten gains and I appeared like a ghost from nowhere, asking if I could be of assistance. I was carrying the paintings under my arm and her face was the best picture of all when she saw them.

At least I stopped taking things at fifteen-years-old and it was all petty stuff, these were people with plenty of money judging by the car they left in. Maybe that's how they get their money.

Stealing isn't the only illegal activity that goes on either. We had converted a few bedrooms above the restaurant into hotel chambers and the moment we opened those, the trade was really busy.

A lady from a model agency rang one day to book a room and told us that she would have her models stay there when they were in the area. Linda was so pleased and the lady checked in on the afternoon of her stay. She definitely looked like a model and she told Linda her boss was arriving to check that the rooms were OK too.

I was standing in the cocktail bar when a bloke in a pin stripe suit came tearing past me on his way out. I asked Linda who he was and she told me it was the model's boss. He was in a hurry and looked like he was running away from something.

A little while later, the lady from the model agency came to Linda and said something had cropped up and she couldn't stay. She paid for the room and Linda was pleased, telling me that she could re-let the room for the night. That's the kind of customer Linda likes.

Something rang a bell in my mind and I told Linda she had better check the room because I thought she looked like a prostitute. Linda and Julie tore up there and sure enough Julie found an empty condom packet in the bathroom bin. Linda was devastated because she is so naive about that sort of thing and we just laughed our heads off at the situation. I hope you understand why I put these stories in, it gives you a feel for the things we have to put up with in the trade.

We aren't immune to making mistakes ourselves so I thought I would tell you a couple of tales about our failings.

One man was eating in the restaurant and spilt some butter over his jacket. He'd done it himself but we tried to help out, the waiter offering to try and sort out the situation for the customer.

The waiter brought the jacket into the kitchen, asking for a spoon which he heated over a naked flame, he told me he had learned this in France and using the hot spoon on the stain would remove it. Whether it did or not was immaterial as the spoon burned a hole straight through the jacket.

He had the unfortunate problem of having to tell the customer what had happened and I just collapsed with laughter. The man went ballistic and we had to compensate him but it was almost worth the money to see the look of panic on the head waiter's face.

Another incident happened to Linda which was similar to the man with the jacket. This time another diner had managed to get grease on his coat and Linda had told him if you put brown paper over it and ironed it, the stain would remove. We couldn't find any brown paper in the restaurant but one of the lads had recently eaten a MacDonald's and the bag was left in the restroom.

That would do, she thought, and started to iron the grease away and in fairness, the stain came out. The only problem when she removed the brown paper bag was a row of McDonald's Ms decorating the coat. Again I collapsed but the man didn't notice what had happened and left the restaurant totally ignorant of his new style of coat.

When you're in a trade like ours, you try and keep the costs down as much as possible and we had problems with a bay window in the restaurant so I called a mate of mine, telling him of the predicament. He told me not to worry and said he knew a couple of lads who would sort out the situation and I could pay them cash in hand.

The window needed waterproofing and the lads were to tar up the holes around the leaded glass sections.

Laurel and Hardy couldn't have been any more inept than the two vagabonds who turned up but I took my friend's assurance that they could do the job when I employed them.

They stoked up the tar container until it bubbled away nicely, with that smell that I love coming from it and then they put their ladder up against the window.

There were six diners just coming to the end of their meal inside the alcove by the bay window and they were looking out at the work being done. One of the two lads got a pail of tar and climbed the ladder to start the job. As he reached the top rung there was a sickening crack and the window gave way, pitching him through it, with glass showering the guests and the table. The tar went everywhere over the stonework and the drive outside. It took me weeks of patient chipping to get the residue off and, to add insult to injury, I was forced to cancel the diners' bill.

Laurel and Hardy did a runner so that I couldn't pull them about it but a small job cost me a fortune to have put right. In future I would always use someone reputable I decided.

These incidents are part of life in the catering trade. When we left the restaurant business to concentrate on Millers

Catering, we missed all these things, happy or sad, so it was great to be able to open my restaurant and get back into the business.

CHAPTER SIXTEEN

FOOD

The catering industry is notorious for problems or amusing incidents. I am a big bloke with a shaven head, so a lot of people believe I know nothing about food. They look at the packaging, not the man, and it tends to make them think I will just accept anything without knowing what is correct.

There is a very large, well-known and upmarket hotel in the Newcastle area, which has a good reputation for food but I remember once being in their restaurant and ordering surf and turf.

Surf and turf means different things in different establishments but this hotel's boast was a fillet steak accompanied by three king prawns.

When the dish arrived, the plate consisted of the steak, one king prawn and two pieces of monkfish. I know the problems chefs have at times and I would bet that the head chef had run out of king prawns and the waiter had described me to him, saying I would never know the difference.

The chef will have taken the chance and sent what he had but I think the waiter got a bit of a shock when he asked me if everything was OK with the meal. I had left the two pieces of monkfish on the plate and his face was so comical when I said the king prawn had been OK but the monkfish wasn't. I've never seen anyone clear a plate and leave so fast in all my years in the business. The point I'm making here is be very sure that what you order is what you get, most people in England wont complain, I think its something to do with our personalities, but you are entitled to get exactly what you pay for.

It's not just the wrong food being served either. There was the time when I ordered fish and chips in a fairly high quality restaurant. When the fish arrived, the batter was so thick that I could wave it around in the air like a light sabre from Star Wars and it wouldn't break. Obi Wan Kenobi would have been proud of its sturdiness. How something like that escaped from the kitchen I will never know. Sending that kind of stuff out is an embarrassment. Batter is a simple thing to make, fish shop batter only consists of flour, water and a bit of vinegar and lemon juice so there really is no excuse to get it wrong.

No kitchen is immune from situations like this. In one restaurant I owned, one of my own chefs cooked fifty chickens with the plastic bag of giblets still inside the birds. It's a damned good job that I always check the food before it is served or we could have been in serious trouble that day.

Customers can cause you frustration where food is concerned too, especially regulars. A man who shall remain anonymous used to have breakfast everyday in a hotel where I was employed. He told me when he first arrived that he always ate a full English breakfast, so for seven days straight I would cook him his preference and everyday he came into breakfast telling me he had changed his mind and only wanted a couple of poached eggs on toast. He was lucky he didn't have poached egg earmuffs for that stunt. As a result, the calories went straight down my throat, not the best of ideas for a man who struggles with his weight. Most of us do it, cook a few sausages, bacon, mushrooms etc just to give us a head start in the morning and what's left the staff usually eat. It's a good excuse to have breakfast.

Diners can cause you a lot of trouble in a restaurant environment, just by being obnoxious. You get the professional complainers, who don't have anything better to do in their lives but pick fault, so food is a good area to moan about.

I've had a lot of those over the years but one I can remember vividly was a peroxide blonde who had seen better days. She was the worst type of whinger who needed everyone in the place to know her grumble. These types of people always want to be the centre of attention and try to belittle the staff.

At the end of the restaurant I would display a meal when it was a busy night, mainly seafood so that people could see and choose the dish they were going to get. I went to talk to the woman in question out of politeness and asked her what she thought of the display, when she poured her drink over the arrangement, asking me what I thought of that.

She certainly didn't like it when I grabbed the scruff of her neck and frogmarched her out of the place. Maybe I shouldn't have done it but the applause from everyone in the restaurant showed me how popular she had been.

Anyone who has a genuine complaint will be looked after by me to the utmost of my ability but if anybody makes a complaint which is unjustified, they had better wear their crash helmet. I won't put up with moaning for the sake of moaning. Over the years, I have come to realise that some people just spoil their own night for no reason at all.

It really hacks me off that some diners come in with the intention of finding something wrong, so that you will either waive the bill or give them something extra to compensate when there is nothing wrong with their food in the first place. I don't know how they have the gall to do it. It's nothing but robbery and an absolute disgrace.

A chef doesn't even need to be wrong to get it in the ear. Burns Night suppers are very impressive nights and I enjoy cooking for them but one of my first was a nightmare. The organisers had asked me to be on stage when the address to the haggis was taking place. It's a very impressive piece of prose written by Robert Burns and I apologise to any Scots readers for what I'm about to say.

As the spokesman began the talk, I just couldn't help laughing at the flowery Scots wording. That was a bad start but worse was to follow.

The starter for the evening was the traditional haggis, neeps and tatties and that was fine, a main course of steak pie had been ordered to follow. As a rule, you would have potatoes with the pie but one of the women from the group informed me that no potatoes would be needed as they had already been served with the starter.

I wish she had told the man in overall charge because he took me outside and ripped into me. I think he told me I was a fucking, useless, stinking, bastard and that he would make sure I never worked in Newcastle again. In fact, if it was up to him, I would never work in England again. As I stood there smiling at him, I don't think it helped the situation as he looked like he might explode at any moment. He was like a manic Basil Fawlty on speed.

A lot of grumbles are like that. If people would only check with their parties, they might find that a lot of problems could be sorted out without making a complaint. It didn't affect me professionally but it could have.

Whenever I interview a chef, I always ask the same question and it's amazing how many potential employees get it wrong. I simply ask what the difference is between shepherd's and cottage pie. The answer is one is made from beef and the other from lamb but you would be amazed how many people get tongue tied when trying to answer that simple question.

It's not rocket science and it's amazing how many backsides are like the speed of a rocket as they leave the interview in embarrassment. At interview, I always tell the candidates that my signature dish is King Prawn Rockafella and ask them what theirs is. If they answer steak and chips, they definitely aren't for me.

I'm not free from mistakes myself and I would be the first to admit that, but once in a while you have to be economical with the truth. In the pub we had a very important wedding. They're all important, I know, but this one was particularly special and we had spent a lot of time making sure the place was immaculate.

On the evening before the big day, the bride's mother dropped off the most beautiful three-tier wedding cake which had been decorated to perfection, pristine white icing covered it and I decided to place it in the fridge overnight for safekeeping.

When I took it out the next day, the cake looked like it had jaundice. The icing had yellowed and I mean yellowed. It was the same shade as a banana. Panic set in at this point but Linda told me not to worry, in fact she dimmed the lights and closed the curtains. The bride's mother noticed the mistake later that day and I blamed the person who iced the cake telling her the icing was too thin but it was still a beautiful cake.

Weddings do give you a particular problem, like the time we had a groom who invited the world to his wedding at his stag night the day before. Just come down, he said, and they did, in droves. Over a hundred extra guests arrived on the day but we managed to feed them. Mind you, it's lucky for him that he left for Portugal on his honeymoon before I finished the service. If he hadn't, it might have been the shortest marriage on record.

Food over the last twenty years or so has been a bit of a hot potato and very controversial. It all started with Edwina Currie, who told everyone about salmonella in eggs and she lost her job because she brought the situation out into the open.

In my view, she was right to bring the matter up. Two close friends of mine contracted poisoning from eggs and were left in a disastrous state of health because of it.

Whenever I buy eggs now, whether for my business or home use, I always make sure that I purchase the highest quality that I can. It's not an absolute guarantee of salmonella-free stock but as I always say, FRESH MEANS BEST.

If I watch television pictures of the way chickens are cramped into cages, with nothing else to do but produce, it really sickens me to the stomach. The food I use must be right and the best I can get. Seeing those birds hemmed in, trying to find some space to move makes my blood boil. Talking like this as a chef won't do me any favours in the industry but just because I own a restaurant doesn't mean that I have to turn a blind eye to these kinds of factory farm methods.

Slaughter techniques are repulsive too. I have only once witnessed the killing of animals in an abattoir and I hope I never see or hear anything like it ever again. There is one thing you will never see on my menus, veal. It was a great seller at his previous place, as one of my chefs keeps telling me and that is great, but if he is so keen on it, he can go back there. When I said that to him the first time, he thought I was kidding. I wasn't and he knows how strongly I feel about it now.

I can't understand what has happened in the last couple of decades. We've had salmonella, CJD, worms in salmon, botulism and any amount of other general food poisoning germs coming to the fore, all this at a time when hygiene procedures have supposedly been tightened up.

Isn't it amazing then, that I can remember a time before mass refrigeration in homes, when all that we had was a pantry and a marble slab to store our food on. There were nowhere near as many incidents of food poisoning then as I remember.

In those days, we had seasonal food but now you can get most food items all year round. It makes me wonder if there is something wrong in all this because they are grown on forced spraying of chemicals and lacquers for presentation.

The consumer is driving prices down but low prices mean producers usually have to cut corners somewhere and food is the last area where any reduction of attention should take place.

One supermarket may be selling a chicken for £4 and right next door the same one is going for £3. You don't have to be a genius to know that somewhere, something has to give to get that decrease in price. Is it imported beef or chicken, that's what you have to ask yourself?

Restaurants are involved with this price war mentality too, with their two for one deals and happy hours. It will never happen but I would love to see us all get together and bring a halt to this cut-throat attitude.

A fair price for a fair product would be beneficial to all restaurant owners and we would be able to ensure the finest, freshest food and ingredients for our customers and standards of producing would rocket.

I am a bit of a traditionalist where cooking and food is concerned, the basics are my favourite foods. Give me a blackberry or raspberry rather than a paw paw or lychee any day. Leg of lamb or a ham joint excite me, much more than the ostrich or wild boar which are coming onto the market these days. Mind you, if I go out for a meal and something exotic is on the menu I have never tried before, I will go for it.

There was a menu once which contained jelly fish head and I was expecting a big blob of jelly on the plate but what came looked like a pile of onions. I'm not a cockly person but the first mouthful started me retching.

Linda had her fork in the dish to try it and I couldn't speak so just slapped her hand to stop her. I managed to put my mouthful into a napkin, telling her I had just saved her life. When the waiter arrived I told him it was disgusting. I don't like to make a fuss but this was appalling, so he took us into the kitchen and everyone there tried it. The expressions on their faces told the story. They told me that they didn't know where the chef's head was when he put the dish on the menu.

The day when government took free school milk out of education was a seriously bad move to me. Youngsters need good calcium from the earliest years and I'm sure if it was reintroduced, kids would benefit from it and there would be fewer instances of osteoporosis in future generations of older women, it's a ticking time bomb for the health service. Government will take away the price of a bottle of milk but is happy to cost the country dear in unhealthier citizens.

As far as my house is concerned, I make sure everyone sits down to a Sunday lunch. I think everyone can sacrifice their computer games, television or other interests to sit with the family and talk about the week. The way kids are allowed to avoid family interaction these days is scandalous. My children are much older now and they have their binges on a Saturday night but they know they must be sitting around that table however they feel at 1pm on a Sunday. I'll use a guilt trip if I need to by telling them that I've worked all week and you lazy sods won't even move to eat what I've made. It usually does the trick.

In some ways I think we've gone too far with food, the consumer must get confused by some of the terms used like eggplant rather than aubergine or zucchini instead of courgette. T.V. chefs and supermarkets are equally to blame for these snobbish changes of name.

Even I am confused at some of the terms used. I can buy

a recipe book and find it difficult to use, so how can the poor consumer cope?

Trends go much further than that though. A few days before I wrote this section, I read a recipe about a man who was cooking squirrels' hearts on a skewer. How sick is that?

One of the weirdest things I have ever seen is a chef making mashed potato and using a temperature probe to ensure the texture was just right. I called it scientific mash and I just wonder what the problem with Smash is.

During my catering training, I worked in some scruffy and low life dives and the things I saw frightened me to death. There were places which would turn the unsold beef and chicken from the previous day into curry or day-old salmon into fishcakes. To cover the tastes and smells they would add so much spice to the dishes that customers couldn't tell the age or unsuitability of the food. I always tell my staff they are never to serve any food that they wouldn't be prepared to eat themselves. It's one of my kitchen mottos and woe betide anyone who disobeys me on that.

If something doesn't look right or smells unusual, they are instructed to bin it immediately. The health of the public is paramount in our business and we've all seen the news stories about people falling ill through bad cooking and hygiene practices.

As a chef, I have eaten things which I haven't been happy about. On one occasion I was eating a croque monsieur (toasted sandwich) in a restaurant and the moment I tasted it, I knew something was amiss so stopped eating.

As I was dining with the owner, she asked me what was wrong with the dish and instead of telling her I wasn't happy, I began picking at it. If you had seen the state of the person who made and served it, I'm sure you would never have eaten it yourself but I felt a bit pressured.

If I had eaten that sandwich, I am convinced I would have died. As it was, I was as ill as I have ever been. From that moment in time I told myself that I would never eat anything again that I wasn't happy with and I have stuck to that.

When I'm in a restaurant and the food reeks or is inedible, I tell the owners immediately. I used to be a big softy but not anymore. Some restaurant owners have no idea about food. Whenever I see Environmental Health Officers checking top establishments, where the staff are obviously trying to keep their premises in tip top condition and then miss out on some of the questionable late night take away food establishments which don't have a licence, it makes me bloody livid.

To illustrate my point, I will tell you a little story about the attitude of a man I knew who owned a fish and chip shop, it shows you how these people view the general public.

The shop he owned was filthy by anybody's standards and he told me that he had changed to making and selling pizzas because the British public were thick. They wouldn't accept paying more than £3.50 for fish and chips or £2.50 for a burger but they would pay £6.00 for a pizza and he could make one of those for 38p. I'm not surprised he could, they are only bread with some tomato puree and a topping of a few bits of meat or vegetables. It wasn't what he could do which bothered me, it was the breathtaking contempt for the public and his laughing at ripping them off which bugged me.

He had a flash Mercedes, Rolex and some nice clothes so it must have done him some good; he'd gone from a miserable scruff to a man with a totally different outlook on life.

The stress generated in a pub restaurant environment can be every bit as intense as the finest restaurants in the land. Mother's Day at the pub for instance saw us cooking and serving three hundred meals from noon to three o'clock, plates were leaving the kitchen at two a minute and the pressure on the staff was enormous.

A young waiter we had was obviously coping badly with the whole thing, you can either stand the heat or you can't and he couldn't. Having me bawling and shouting at him to get the food out didn't help either.

At one point he picked up some plates and headed upstairs to the dining room to serve. As he reached the top step the unfortunate lad dropped a gammon steak on the floor. If he was upset before he was devastated now. The wrath of the chefs was too much to take so he promptly picked up the meat, replaced it on the plate and served it to the customer.

Unfortunately, the diner who ordered it saw the whole thing and rightly refused the dish, telling the waiter he had seen the plate drop, actually he was laughing about it.

The waiter chose to deny that he had done anything wrong, he certainly wasn't going to come and tell me about it so he stuck rigidly to his denial. It got to the stage where the assistant restaurant manager became involved. His dining room was full, there was this complaint to handle and he was juggling about twenty things to do at the same time. To cut a long story short, the manager broke down and we found him sitting on the stairs crying his eyes out like a child. It was pure frustration and no matter how much comfort we tried to give him, he couldn't come out of it. That shows you how much stress a restaurant generates for everyone working there.

One of the loveliest ladies ever was Princess Diana. On the morning of her tragic death I was up early prepping for the day's cooking at the same restaurant when I turned on the radio and heard the reports about a royal death.

At the time, I didn't hear the name and assumed it was the Queen Mother. I rushed upstairs to tell Linda who was still in bed but had to go back later to tell her it was the Princess.

For me Diana was a breath of fresh air to the monarchy, I've thought them far too stuffy for a long time and she brought a real sense of fun to the establishment. Whether you believe she was killed purposely or not, she is a dreadful miss to the country and the world with her fantastic support of causes like AIDS and land mine issues. In my view, she was a REAL Princess of the people.

There is no humour to be had out of a situation like that but just to give you an idea how I can get things wrong I told Linda once that they thought the Princess had been killed by MFI and she asked if they had dropped a wardrobe on her. Of course I meant MI5 but that's me.

Lester on Pride of Pendle.

Alex – The first woman jockey to ride in the Derby.

Dazzler and me.

On top of the world.

Apres Ski

Our little treasure Will – with dad Billy Hardy and me

Everybody's got to start somewhere.

The team

Will and Julie.

Gary me and Alan at the opening of Rockafella's.

CHAPTER SEVENTEEN

PRIDE OF PENDLE

Next to cooking, my greatest passion is horse racing. There's no feeling like standing next to those white rails, waiting for a mass of thundering horses approaching the winning post. The ground literally trembles with the weight of so many horses bunched together, all vying for position.

Sods of earth are churned from the ground, covering the trailing jockeys in spattered patterns, concealing the multicoloured silks in fine brown spots. The magnificent animals snort with nostrils wide as they strive to win the race.

The punters begin a crescendo of encouragement as they urge on the animals, hoping to win a few bob in some cases, a massive amount in others. It's still a true sport which brings the classes together with the same hopes and dreams.

Finally, they pour past the post, usually with the winning jockey holding his whip high in the air and the shouting dies down slowly from the crowd.

From an early age I had watched horse racing on T.V.

with my dad and brother Richard. Every Saturday morning would be taken up with conversation about who was likely to win that afternoon's races and needless to say the chat would continue into Sunday with all the, 'If only's'.

Even though I always tried to persuade them to put a bet on for me, my dad restricted me to Grand National day while they would bet on most big race days. I loved the sport and I adored the animals, so sleek and turned out in wonderful fashion by the stable lads.

A lot of you would say that gambling in that fashion would lead to severe problems today and, to be fair, you could be right but my dad and brother only ever bet coppers and usually on multiples for a better chance of a bigger pay day.

Even today, I love betting on a multiple and for ten or twenty pounds you can win a fortune. The chances of one of the multiples coming up is rare but every now and again you get lucky.

I can remember the day I was sucked into racing as a regular passion. It was 1967 and a 100/1 shot called Foinavon won the National. The fence after Bechers was one of the smallest on the track but for some reason horses got tangled and they almost all fell. Foinavon was so far back that he missed the havoc and went on to win the great race. To this day I can still conjure up that race in my mind and will always remember Foinavon and the second horse, Honey End, which my mam had backed.

My dad only went to the races once, many years after the Foinavon National. He was never a bloke for that kind of thing. When I think about it now, he never even brought a mate home from work and yet there were hundreds there at his funeral. This one time he went racing on a trip with the lads to Thirsk in North Yorkshire on Hunt Cup day there and it's still one of Yorkshire's most prestigious meetings. Before he went, Richard marked up the paper for him that day and he had five winners out of the six races. I wish I'd been there to see the expression on his face.

When he got home, I was in bed so I never saw him that night either but the next morning he had a grin on his face from ear to ear and he slipped me a few bob. It was one of the best days I saw him smile. I wish there could have been more towards the end of his life.

My brother Richard has always been a good tipster, studying form and making sure his money was safe as best he could. Over the years we've been to the races together quite a few times and he has helped me make more than a few bob regularly.

It was while we were involved in renovating a hotel in Whitley Bay the opportunity to get closer to the horse racing fraternity in a bigger way came about. We'd been offered a hotel by one of the breweries while at the pub and were halfway through the building work when a couple of entrepreneurs wanted to buy it from us, so we agreed and the deal was done. The agreement was they would pay half now and half when they signed for the premises and that would be paid on a weekly basis.

Up to that point, money had been tight so we couldn't believe our luck. Linda's first thought was a shopping expedition or a car, which she got, but for myself I knew what I wanted, my own racehorse. The question was, how to go about it?

Luckily, I knew a customer who was a good friend to a

trainer, he made a couple of calls and before I knew it, I was on my way to the sales.

When we got there, I couldn't believe my eyes. Kevin Keegan and his wife were there too, running the rule over some horses themselves. She is a breeder and had a wonderful stallion.

The sights and sounds of that day will remain with me always. I couldn't believe the amount of quality horses on show and the number of people bidding for them. Even if we found something, I knew it could cost us dearly but what the hell, it was a chance I wasn't going to pass up.

I was a bit overawed by the whole thing but as we sat with the trainer, a beautiful young grey filly appeared in the showing ring. Linda's eyes had that, 'I want this' look and I knew what was going to happen. It's the same look she has when shopping and I can't deny her anything. I wouldn't even like to try and deny her. The horse had already won a couple of races that year and I couldn't understand why the owner would want to sell a successful horse. If it had been my horse, I would have wanted to keep her for another year. Some horses develop hidden problems in racing so I was being cautious about her.

Linda was bidding and the price was rising five hundred guineas a time. She was biting the inside of her lip, so I knew she was deadly serious. Finally the hammer went down to Linda at fifteen thousand guineas and Linda had got her way once again.

The horse was the most expensive that day and her name was Pride of Pendle. She was to become like a member of the family and even when I speak her name now, I get goose bumps on the back of my neck. The animal means the world to me and she was so placid in character that I wondered what we had done at the time but I needn't have worried. Linda brought out a packet of Polo's to feed the horse and with a few gentle scratches, Pride of Pendle was closing her eyes on the verge of sleep, with her head under Linda's coat sleeve. It was just a great day all round and I couldn't wait to see her run. Linda named her Poppy.

The trainer told us we had to wait until the following season to race her at her best so it was a frustrating time for me. That first race had to be on my home turf so we entered her for a meeting in Newcastle. All our friends and relatives came to see her that day and I was bursting with pride.

As we watched her race that day, I didn't feel the jockey was doing her any favours, she was trapped on the rails and he didn't seem to be able to get her away from them. She finished down the field but we had a great time and still thought she was lovely. Our kid used to say I was watching her through rose-tinted spectacles but you know what, I didn't care. She was ours and we loved her, whatever she did. It was a while later that Linda and I decided that our trainer needed to be changed as the horse didn't seem to be fulfilling her potential. There was a trainer I had been keeping note of, who had been having a lot of success on all-weather tracks with very ordinary horses. He was called Dandy Nichols.

I thought the switch would do Pendle good so I approached the man and couldn't believe my eyes. All he had was a big hangar-style barn, a couple of fields and he was living in a caravan, but what he lacked in luxury, he more than made up for in spirit. When I saw how he loved and treated his horses, I was sure he was the man for us.

For many years, he had been a successful flat jockey but

creeping weight gain put a stop to his career. Dandy told me that he jogged six miles a day with a bin bag covering his skin so that he could take off the pounds when he was racing. He and his wife, Alex, are a really lovely couple and we had great times with them.

On the day I took the horse from the first trainer, he was a bit bitter and wouldn't release her until he was paid and that was fair enough I suppose. I remember counting out a sizeable amount for him on the bonnet of the car and at the same time, thinking that he didn't deserve it.

Over the weeks, she had a few more runs with little success, when Linda asked if we could run her at the Ascot of the North, York. Everyone laughed at her, thinking she was so naive and telling her that they were sorry love but you don't know anything about horses. That attitude really doesn't go down well with Linda but the trainer told her, only the best horses go to York and it wouldn't do the horse any good. It would cost a fortune to get her in he said. You've probably gathered that Linda has her own mind and she just told him to give it a try, no matter what the cost. She knew, if the horse got in the handicap she would be able to run.

We booked into the racecourse hotel so we could really enjoy the day and at least have a few drinks. The day before, our trainer asked who Linda wanted to ride Pride of Pendle and she automatically asked for Frankie Dettori. The stunned look on his face was a picture when he told her that she didn't want much but five minutes later he rang back, astonished, to say he had got him.

I was beside myself with excitement and I stayed up all night ringing around people to tell them the news. My brother Richard still thought we were nuts and would get a real showing up.

As I looked out over the course that day, I thought how proud my dad would have been.

Channel Four were covering the race on T.V. so anyone left in the North East could watch it but we decided to watch from next to the winning post with the big screen opposite. The tension was unbearable as we saw the first half of the race unfold. Two furlongs from home, Frankie burst through the field. All I could see was a grey coming into shot so I knew it was her and shouted, "She's coming Linda, she's coming." As I said that, she went clear, everyone at home would be cheering I knew, and my mam told me a couple of days later that my brother nearly shouted the house down. It meant so much to me that our Richard would be in his element about it because he just loves the sport so much. As she flashed by the post, Linda and I were in tears. She had been right all along, not only had she won, she had hacked up. There's few times I have felt that proud in all my life.

As Frankie brought the horse to the edge of the course, we went to see her and he asked us if we were the owners. When Linda told him yes, he told us to take the reins and guide her to the winner's enclosure. As we walked her along, the cameras followed our every step. We were the proudest people on the planet at that great moment.

Pride of Pendle won three more races that year and in the others, if she was beaten it was normally a close second or third.

Our lives were taken over by horse racing heaven, Linda was on T.V. being interviewed a lot and people stopped us in the streets to ask about the horse.

At the end of that season, we decided she needed a good

long rest because she deserved it and that's what we did. The trainer told us she only needed a couple of runs to get fit so he didn't need to work her much at the stables.

The next season was on us fast and I wanted the horse to run in the Thirsk Hunt Cup, which was the meeting my dad had been to previously. If I'm honest about it, that was only a dream and I couldn't believe it when we were on our way to race there. Prize money for the race was a cool £15,000 but more important for me, remembering my dad, was winning the prestigious cup. All of my thoughts about this race centred around him, winning it was that important to me.

There were two greys in the race, Queen's Counsel and my beloved Pride of Pendle and at four furlongs from home Queen's Counsel was out in front clear and no one could surely beat her.

My jockey was the trainer's wife, Alex Greaves, who was the first woman jockey to ride in the Derby. Pendle gave chase and in the final furlong she was flying. As the line grew closer she got up by a neck and had won. I was crying and every emotion in my body was on fire. Before the race had started, I looked into the crowd where I felt I could see my fathers smiling face and when Pendle crucified the field, I took a few seconds out to look for him among the people. I knew he wasn't there but it was one time I really believed in God.

No matter how important or rich the race was, I always told the jockeys that they were never to use the whip if she was clearly beaten and even then just a couple of gentle flicks. That's all it needed with Pendle and she would motor on from just those gentle promptings.

The presentation of the cup was a blur. I was completely out of it but the next day I took the cup down to my mam's and put it on the top of her T.V. It started my mam crying and my brother Richard hugged me tight, I knew how much it meant to both of them.

Pendle is retired now, after a fantastic career, so we sent her to a stud farm in Ireland. When we had her, the money dried up from the hotel but she always paid for herself winning good prizes all year round. Even when money was non existent for Linda and me, I kept Pendle because I couldn't let her down. She had given us so much pleasure that I couldn't let her fall into the hands of some wrongdoer who would treat her badly.

The foals Pendle has produced are fantastic too and I kept the first one which looks the spitting image of her mother. She's won a couple of races, with the same heart as her illustrious parent.

Pride is eighteen-years-old now and the fourteen years we have had her have just flown by. She has given us so much joy and when people say money can't buy happiness, it's wrong because that is just what she did.

I met my best mate Darren at the races and he will always be my best mate. We don't see or telephone each other much but there is that bond two blokes have between them which a woman would never understand. I've nicknamed him Dazzler because he is 6ft 3in tall, tanned all over and a really big bloke.

When Frankie Dettori won his famous seven races on the same day, Darren was the only man in the country who backed him to do it with £50. He won half a million from that, so that was a good day's multiple.

The racing business has given me much to be thankful for and I hope it always will. The day that Alex Nichols ran in the Derby was a special day for us too. We had stayed with the Nichols' for the week during the build up to the great race and reporters and TV media were interviewing Alex everywhere she went.

On the morning of the Derby, Dandy invited Linda and me to walk the course with him while he carried out his observations. Other trainers like Sheik Mohamed, the sovereign's trainer, and most of the other major trainers were walking the turf in packs and there was I, a big Geordie boy doing the same. I was so proud that day. You may not notice on T.V. but the course slopes toward the rails drastically which forces the horses to favour their left legs and pushes them into the rails, the camber is so pronounced.

Dandy is one of the biggest trainers in England now but I will never forget meeting him in his humble caravan, watching over his horses in the fields and looking after them like a dedicated trainer should. The days we had together may never come again but the debt we owe him and his lovely wife Alex where Poppy is concerned is something we will never be able to repay.

CHAPTER EIGHTEEN

THE FRENCH CONNECTION

I f there is one thing in life I truly despise, it's the package holiday. I like being in control when I'm on a break, so I hate the holiday reps on package trips being in charge and planning out what I will be doing. It's not my idea of fun.

When I choose holiday destinations, I always look for areas where food plays a big part in the region, so France is one of the countries for me.

My friends are flabbergasted when I tell them I'm going there. They all think the French are an arrogant bunch of arseholes but I've always found them to be a friendly bunch, always helpful and attentive. I really can't believe their attitude; it seems they pigeonhole every French person as being that way. How blinkered is that? Not once in all the times I've been there, have I come across that kind of outlook so I'm going to tell it the way I feel it, I LIKE THE FRENCH and I always speak as I find.

When we get home and want to share the experiences with friends, they just don't want to know about our travels there.

The first couple of times I visited the country, we toured in a caravan to the Loire and then the Alps. There are no words to describe the beauty of those regions and I felt so at home as a chef travelling through towns and villages named after cheeses I'd used for years but had no real idea of the wonderful districts they came from. As a chef, the thrill of experiencing those places was awesome. They had only been names on a packet before and there I was seeing the scene and talking the talk with the locals in places like Pont Le Veque and Camembert.

I always drive the scenic routes when I'm there which used to drive Graeme, Anthony and Julie mad. Like most kids, they wanted me to use the motorways and get to the destination as fast as possible but I was determined to see as much rural scenery as I could. It caused a few lively discussions and I would tell them that these routes were the real France. From the moment we got in the car all they would say was, are we there yet?

Routes to France are so easy and regular these days on hovercraft or ferry via Dover to Calais or Portsmouth to St. Malo. In fact, the hardest part of the trips for me is the drive between Newcastle and the South coast.

The cockneys are a lucky bunch. If I lived down in that part of the country, I would be across to France every weekend, I love it that much.

Years ago, we would see French onion sellers in the North East but they died out a long time ago and by using the back roads in France I can still see them, cycling slowly along with their berets and that laid back attitude we would do well to copy over here.

I'm always amazed at the dense, tree lined back roads I

see over there, where the canopies meet over the tarmac in continuous green arches. The effect is stunning. Chateaux rising above hillsides covered in teeming vineyards, give a real sense of the Gallic history.

To get an even better feel, I have taken bikes with me, using them to take a leisurely glimpse at the countryside. On one occasion, the big Geordie was puffing along trying to give the impression of the cool regular cyclist, when a bunch of seasoned bikers passed me as though they were on motorbikes. I don't think the milk racers have anything to worry about where I'm concerned so I won't be taking that up as a career.

Linda and I used to love to just travel from village to village with no set pattern, we just let the flow take us. Once we were sheltering along the side of a building during a thunderstorm, when a little old woman came out of a nearby house and ushered us inside her home. They even allowed us to bring our bikes into the hallway. The husband appeared with a bottle of wine and poured glasses for everyone.

My French is non existent and we found out pretty quickly that their English wasn't much good either, so communication was impossible. It was like a friendly waxworks in that room. Everyone just sat looking and smiling with a bit of drinking mixed in. Sign language saved us; it's amazing how you can communicate when you want to.

Drinking plays a massive part of visiting wine caves in France, you have to be really careful when they begin their free wine tasting. The trouble is, they can be extravagant with the amount. After half an hour in the first cave, you're halfway drunk and by the time you've visited a dozen of them, it's time to leave the car where you parked it, if you can remember where that is, of course.

At every cave we visit, we buy at least one bottle and most times we buy a case based on the taste we've had, but I always thought the wine we tasted in situ was better than the bottles we brought home. It may be something to do with being there I suppose.

Down through the Loire, you come across the Troglodyte villages, where the small houses are cut haphazardly into the hillsides. They have been turned into mushroom caves now, very damp and smelly, but people used to live in them in the dim, distant past. The ceilings are very low so the occupants must have been tiny. I may not seem like the kind of bloke who likes scenery and history when you first see me but I am. Those kinds of things fascinate me.

The mushrooms I saw looked like works of art, the way they had grown naturally into bizarre shapes and are cheap as chips to buy there, but massively expensive here in the UK. One of the varieties was called black trumpet and I've never tasted anything like it to this day.

Going on towards the Alps, we would visit any side markets, where they still to this day sell live birds in cages. That really upset me, having had a kestrel when I was young. I knew I shouldn't have kept that hawk, so ever since then caged birds have been a bit of a hobby horse of mine.

The food in these regions is magnificent too, cheese crepes and gallettes in particular. Linda and the kids like the sweet crepe pancake but my favourite is the savoury gallette filled with ham and cheese and one of my other preferences is the gauffe which is a type of waffle. I love them with ice cream and chocolate.

The Alps wasn't my scene at all. It was far too

commercial for me with its mountain biking, mini golf and cable car rides. Great for kids letting their hair down for a day but it was time to move on so we left very quickly.

We knew we weren't far from Italy and decided to cross the border for a change and to experience a bit of the country. It was red hot and we found a beach where the kids could play, while the adults had a bit of relaxation.

Whenever possible, I travel in the evening to avoid the baking heat of the day. The caravan we were using was located in a car park close to the beach and after a couple of hours lazing on the sand I went back alone to get a flask of tea and to make some sandwiches. I had been wandering around with a cool box and flask the whole holiday so the kids were comparing me to Homer Simpson. On this occasion, I had left it because the kids had been taking the piss.

The moment I got to the caravan I knew instinctively that something was wrong. Walking around the back I noticed that the window had been broken and the caravan had been rifled. Thinking they might still be in there, I burst in, in a rage. It's instinct when someone invades your life I suppose. The whole place had been turned upside down. Clothes, money, jewellery and a camera with two week's holiday snaps had all been taken. If I'd gotten the thieves at that moment I would have killed them.

Linda and the kids blamed me of course because it had been my idea to visit Italy in the first place but Linda was smiling when she said, "You and your bloody Italy." We tried asking for directions to the police station from some people on the beach but communication was difficult. I was happy to just put it all behind us but Linda had paid a lot of insurance premium and insisted we report the incident and she was right.

The police station was on the crest of a hill at the top of a winding road and it looked like a box with a prison door and a hatch on it for an entrance. Linda knocked on the door, the hatch opened and a man's face appeared, then it shut just as quickly and she stood around thinking the door would open but it didn't. She knocked a few times and got a mouthful of something not very nice in Italian.

Linda got sick and came to get me, thinking I might have better luck. I knocked and the same face appeared at the hatch but this time he smiled and opened the door. I was ushered in and tried to tell him what had happened to us but he said something about football and his team, Lazio. He wasn't interested in the tale about the caravan at all, he just said 'sit' and then got on the phone.

About an hour later, through which time he smiled at me constantly, a young lad in his twenties appeared. Although he looked Italian, it turned out that he was from North Shields and was a recruit in the Italian police. The bloke who had rung him was his superior and had told him to get his arse to the station as he thought he had Paul Gascoigne with him.

The young lad had to break it to him that I wasn't Gazza but came from Newcastle too and supported United. To get his boss to look into the robbery, I told him I was one of Paul Gascoigne's relations. He was delighted, bringing me tea and sandwiches and he managed to get the caravan window a temporary repair. We made our way back into France with yet another holiday story to our name.

We headed for Gauge De Verdon and drove through a mountain range via the Napoleon Pass and I've never seen a sight like it. If you can imagine a mini version of the Grand Canyon then you have an idea of its stunning splendour.

The area has man-made lakes and I took the kids for a swim in them. As we paddled about, my feet touched the bottom and sank into black silt. It was enough to start us mud fighting and the kids and myself looked a sight when I took them back to Linda. Needless to say she wasn't pleased.

Unfortunately, it was Gauge De Verdon where I first saw horsemeat on a menu. I looked around at the diners' plates who were eating it, feeling so sad that one of the kindest animals on the planet was being served as a delicacy.

I've already said that Linda and I know very little French so we always buy an English version guidebook to find our way around. We had the opportunity to visit France once without the kids. It was intended to be a romantic few days together and we selected a chateau and some other unusual venues to stay.

The guide books were always spot on with their descriptions of locations to visit like Dinan or Honfleur which were just photographs to us in the past. Now we could see them in their glory and they were breathtaking. I've always had a real soft spot for nice places so this was my idea of heaven.

We found a really picturesque restaurant on the bank of a river in one of these villages and Linda ordered fois gras with a port sauce which looked outstanding. She still talks about that evening regularly, a real sentimental night with everything perfect, something that only happens a few nights in the whole of your life. Mind you, I tell her that everyday is Valentine's Day in our house.

The following day, we went shopping in Deauville which

is a very upmarket town, spending part of the day at the Deauville horse race meeting. It was a great day for English trained winners and I was lucky enough to come away with a good few bob in my pocket.

Deauville is situated on the coast and is known as the city of the horse, judging by the way they looked after the animals at the race meeting, you can see why. When we left Deauville, we decided to travel further along the coast for a couple of hours. Like Northumberland, the beaches are fantastic but different in many ways and are very dangerous due to the Atlantic rollers hitting them. The sea is inviting but I could imagine some tragic accidents if people weren't aware of the hazards.

Linda had thoroughly enjoyed the fois gras which she had eaten on our family holiday the night before so she was delighted when we stopped at a restaurant overlooking the sea and saw the same dish on the menu. As fate would have it, she ordered it again when the chef came to see us. She explained to him that her dish the night before had been garnished with port sauce which she found an excellent accompaniment so he told her to leave it to him.

When you try to relive something, it never quite works out. The meal was very good but the emotion of the previous night wasn't quite as intense this time.

We needed somewhere to stay and checked the guide book which mentioned an impressive chateau but it seemed far too expensive. There were a lot of places in the book priced between £30 - £50 but everything was fully booked so the chateau was a last resort.

It certainly was imposing but all they had available was the wing where Louis X1V had stayed. From the King of

France to the Geordie Rockafella, would the chateau be the same again? The price was a little more than £30 a night at a mere £160 but sometimes you have to have a bit of luxury. It's not everyday you sleep in the turret where Louis X1V slept so we just thought, go for it.

The place was just perfect and I started to think about a little romance but that was knocked on the head very quickly when Linda began to feel unwell. At first we thought it might be a bit of travel sickness but halfway through the night the food poisoning kicked in.

All night she clung to Louis' bog with her head permanently down it. All I could do was sit next to her with a wet towel trying to mop her brow of that horrible cold sweat you get when vomiting.

All the next day she slept, just out of it with the illness. If I could have got a hold of that bastard chef, I would have killed him. We hung on there for two days until Linda was well enough to travel but even then she wasn't eating and was still feeling ill.

Angers was a large town which we visited next and I had hoped that she would be feeling a lot better but that wasn't the case. I'm not being selfish here but when your partner isn't well; the holiday isn't even half as enjoyable. You want to eat and drink together and there I was having to do that alone with Linda just smiling at me over a glass of water. It really upset me that she was so bad and that our holiday was being spoilt by some stupid caterer. I can tell you now, the holiday is never the same when that happens.

I bought a French phrase book while we were there and Linda was unwell and asleep and started to study it. When she woke she was pleasantly surprised and laughed at my little sayings. Hoping she was starting to get back on her feet again, I told her I thought I was a real Francophile; it was just an attempt to make her laugh again.

After the bout of serious food poisoning, Linda needed some serious rest so we spent a few days there before going to Cognac and a visit to the Hennessy factory. This was more like it I thought. What an eye opener that place was, with two guards watching over the entrance to a cell which contains 17th century brandy. I watched them to see if they swayed a bit but they must have been conscientious sentries.

I had one or two tipples there before we took a look at the Benedictine church, where the monks toiled to make the stuff. That was a bit of a foody one for me because they displayed all the ingredients and invited visitors to smell each component. I think I surprised the brothers by identifying all the herbs and spices, which we have used over here for years. To say I felt big headed as I left would be an understatement but I wondered if my skull would have any clearance on either side of the door.

The holiday was over and we headed to St. Malo for the boat home. There was a bit of disappointment that we were leaving, despite Linda's horrible food experience. It had been a great time for the most part but all good things have to come to an end. St. Malo is a large walled city which pleasantly surprised me. The seafood there is some of the best you'll find in France. Restaurants buried and hidden from view in sidings in the walls of the town, serve the most amazing three-tier platters for two people. Even though Linda wasn't eating, she couldn't resist it. So that is my take on France, a lovely country with a very friendly people. It may not be the classic English view, but I always speak as I find.

CHAPTER NINETEEN

TALES FROM THE EMERALD ISLES

Ireland is a wonderful place, full of history, beauty and luckily, Guinness. While the writing of this book is taking place, I visited the Emerald Isle with the intention of seeing Pride of Pendle, my racehorse, who was in foal. I love Ireland and its people, the craic there is the best in the world.

The purpose of this chapter is to criticise the hospitality industry in general and NOT Ireland. We have some very good friends in Eire and I would particularly like to mention Catherine and Liam Cashman and their daughter, Niamh at Rathbarry stud who have been so helpful to us. Niamh takes us to the horse sales when we are there and looks after us so well.

In Ireland, we came across many really nice people but there were a few unhelpful ones too, as there is in any country. It doesn't bother me if people are like that these days and I take it all in my stride. A lot of you will have gone through the same problems with people and that's why I've put this short chapter in the book.

Our adventures started at Newcastle Airport at the Bureau De Change, trying to change sterling into euros. No problem, the Bureau was open so we headed towards it and I caught the eye of the teller inside, who immediately looked away from me. At that moment the roller shutter started to descend but I shouted to her to ask if she could help me and she nodded, but the shutter was like a guillotine as it came down and nearly chopped my toes off.

I am no small individual and the moment we took off the guy in front of me reclined his seat. I'm sure that the airlines have a policy of giving the smallest space between seats. When this bloke started putting his seat back, his head kept rubbing on the fabric and I was covered in dandruff of biblical proportions covering me in a generous snowstorm every so often.

When I decided enough was enough, I looked over the aisle where I saw some empty seats so I dived for one of those to avoid anymore human fallout. Good idea, I thought but a real little officious shit of a steward had seen me and ordered me back to my seat. I wouldn't say he was aggressive but he wouldn't have been out of place in the S.S.

The aircraft touched down at Cork Airport and we headed for the rental car we'd reserved, but my wonderful wife had forgotten the voucher which came with the plane tickets. We couldn't remember which hire company we'd booked with and there were several.

The girl at the information desk was very unhelpful, just telling us it had nothing to do with her. She wouldn't let Linda go on the airport website to find her booking so we were forced to go to each rental desk in turn, sounding like idiots when we asked if they had a booking for us.

Of course the queues were massive at each one so we had to stand and, as always happens, the last queue is the one you want. The guy at this one was a really helpful bloke and deserved our business anyway. Being in the hospitality trade attunes us to the helpful and the unhelpful and if the unhelpful ones want to play that sort of game, we can be just as unhelpful back.

Fota Island was the place at which we had booked our hotel. It was a brand new complex and I'm sure it was so new, that no one had slept in our room before us. The room smelled lovely and fresh but there was plaster dust still covering the surfaces - which gave away its recent construction.

Following the trip across we wanted to have a shower and checked the bathroom, but there was no soap or shampoos provided. As it was an expensive establishment, I was annoyed these basic items were missed and I rang down to reception. There were plenty of apologies from the lady on the end of the phone and she told me she would sort it. Half an hour later, I was forced to ring down again only to be told that she was surprised the man with the soap hadn't arrived and she would chase it up again. Fifteen minutes later, there was a knock on the door and I opened it to an empty handed bloke so I asked where the soap was. I couldn't figure out which country he was from and he certainly couldn't understand me so I took him into the bathroom to show him the lack of washing items. Eventually, I got it through to him and he left to get some, bringing them back some minutes later.

It wasn't a good start for this new prestigious hotel and when Linda told me that she couldn't find the hairdryer, it was so ridiculous I started to laugh. Again we rang down and again we had to wait for half an hour and then ring again. Linda was sitting with wet hair all this time. The same guy turned up and rifled the cupboards which we had already done. He then went to get us a hairdryer. It was becoming farcical now and I thought of the money we were spending on this desperately poor service.

At 6.30am the next morning, the icing on the cake came. The previous things had been minor inconveniences but this time we were woken by an engine. I was still half asleep, thinking I was at home with the bin men at work outside but the sound never moved or stopped so I looked out of the window to be faced with a massive crane at work. Now it was getting like Carry On Abroad without the humour.

The familiar sound of workmen's voices, mixed with the revs of the crane as they went about their business, did nothing for a hangover. We were moving on the next morning. All we needed was a Basil Fawlty manager and the hotel would have been complete.

As the receptionist made out the bill for our stay, she asked why we were leaving as we had booked in for four nights. Poor girl, she should have kept her mouth shut and was upset when I told her I had come for a holiday, not work experience. I said it in jokey fashion but she took it to heart when I told her we had come for a rest, not a builders' convention.

Even the leisure facilities weren't open in the hotel so I couldn't imagine why they had started taking guests. It really was a shambles. Her reply to everything was that the hotel wanted guests in to get some feedback on complaints and I think we satisfied their criteria. Why does the hospitality industry allow this kind of thing to go on when it's all so easy to put right?

After all the problems, we didn't feel comfortable using the hotel restaurant so Linda bought a good food guide for the area and we booked an eatery near Clonakilty.

It overlooked the sea front, the guide told us and was renowned for buckets and buckets of my favourite prawns and any fresh seafood you could imagine in abundance. I love the sea and I watched the slate grey waves crash the shore as we ate.

Looking at it when we arrived, it appeared to be like any typical beach hotel in an English seaside resort and Whitley Bay in Northumberland came to mind as we entered. We made up the third table alongside a family of eight who seemed to be like stuffed dummies and another couple, who were equally dull. I was quite surprised because the Irish people we met were very chatty but maybe these were tourists.

Everybody was whispering in that embarrassed fashion, you sometimes do in a strange place and it was a bit like a morgue. When I heard all this whispering going on I wanted to leave but Linda was dressed and we decided to stay. I've been to more interesting funerals and this wasn't my scene.

The whispering was catching and I found myself doing the same as I ordered a prawn cocktail for me and smoked salmon starter for Linda.

When my starter arrived, I looked at it in astonishment. Where the buckets of prawns the guide book had promised, had gone I don't know, but they certainly weren't in my starter. A couple of pathetic looking individuals lay forlornly on a lettuce leaf, accompanied by the thinnest slice of lemon

I've ever seen. God knows what they used to cut it with, probably a Mach3 razor.

My main course was plaice fillets and it's impossible to do anything wrong with that dish, it's flour, batter and fry and is kids' stuff to do. Mine came with the batter peeling off the fish which told me immediately they hadn't dipped the fillets in flour. No wonder the damned place was empty if a seaside resort hotel couldn't get a simple dish like that right. I'm sure they just waited for the next sucker to come along but I'll bet the suckers never ever came back.

To top the dish off, it looked as though it had been splattered on the plate by catapult with an accompaniment of school dinner-style potato and mange tout which was uncooked; it looked like plane crash on a plate.

Linda's prawns and mornay sauce came in a dish that had been standing in an oven or under a grill. The bowl was just a sea of cream with one or two floating shellfish placed in the liquid and then baked. Radiated would have been a better word and when I looked at it, that was all it contained, prawns and cream. The chef must have been one of the most talentless individuals the kitchen trade has ever seen.

I pushed my main down but Linda left hers. As one of the waiters passed, I stopped him to ask where the cheese for the mornay sauce was and he scuttled off to ask the chef. In a game of food hide and seek you would never have found it.

When he came back he asked if we were just passing through or staying in the area and we told him we were booked here for two weeks. What came next was exactly what I knew would come next. His face dropped because he knew he would have to deduct the meal from the bill. If we had told him we were just passing by, I know that he would have insisted we pay for everything. They couldn't afford anyone staying in the area to give out any bad reports about the restaurant so they bit the bullet and deducted the course from the bill.

Going back to the hotel bedroom, we found a polite letter from the hotel management and a lovely present, the bill and a jar of jam. That was a new one on me so I decided the next time I get a complaint in the restaurant, I'll give them a jar of jam - and the bill of course.

At breakfast the next day, we picked at some fruit and orange juice while we waited for my full Irish breakfast and Linda's poached eggs. We waited and we waited and then we waited some more.

Half an hour later, they dropped two plates in front of us with food that must have been cooked at least three hours before, it was wizened and really unappetising. One thing you learn in the trade is the length of time food has been cooked and I know how long the eggs had been prepared and how long it takes for a sausage to go stale. If I had eaten the egg in my Irish breakfast, I know I would have been as ill as Linda was when she got food poisoning on our French trip. How can one day's breakfast be so good and the next days a complete disaster?

Clonakilty and Kinsale were the towns we moved on to next and they were glorious places, particularly Kinsale where there is a scenic harbour, some nice shops, market-style streets and a mass of restaurants and bars.

As we wandered around the town, we came to a small brewery and went inside for a look. The big copper vats were full of the fermenting beer, which gives off an aroma I just love.

Upstairs was a restaurant and I watched the chef go out for a breath of fresh air and five minutes for a coffee. It reminded me of home. I love to talk to people and we had a conversation while he rested and it turned out he was the owner of the place. He gave off the vibe that always tells me, this will be a really good place to eat and I was right again.

That evening we went back to eat there and it was faultless. His style as a chef was really warm too, doing what I do. He came out of the kitchen and visited tables to check everything was OK. When someone sticks their neck out like that, you know they are confident in what they do. His contribution to the holiday made it for us; perhaps it was the chefs bonding thing.

We were coming towards the end of our trip at this point and wanted to see Pendle once more so we travelled back to Rathbarry Stud. When I explained to Catherine what had happened over the holiday, she suggested we stay at a guest house in Conna and recommended it highly.

Her advice was spot on. The place was brilliant and I was delighted to find out that Monty's Pass (the Grand National winner) came from the area. The lady who owned the guest house recognised me from Hell's Kitchen and we sat around talking food for hours, eventually swapping recipes.

I got the greatest surprise when she suddenly asked if we would like to see Monty's Pass. I felt really excited as we pulled up in the car outside the stables with jockeys everywhere and horses blazing along the gallops. It was a typical Irish stable and the jockeys hanging around asked if we would like a bacon sandwich as we waited for the gaffers to come back in.

We sat in the tack room, eating the food among the

evocative smells from the leather saddles and saddle soap, just taking in the atmosphere.

Mrs Mannion brought Monty in to see us and he was a grand soul. It really touched me that they spent a good few hours of their valuable time welcoming us to the place. Stables are busy places at the best of times so the welcome was doubly appreciated. We had a great time in Ireland on the whole but were forced to make our own entertainment as it bucketed down for the entire four days we were there.

Having suffered these problems myself I can understand why the general public go mad with the hospitality trade. Why is the industry going through problems which can so easily be fixed and what is the cause of them? It's beyond me.

CHAPTER TWENTY

TO HELL AND BACK

One evening, Linda, myself and Graeme were sitting watching one of the Gordon Ramsay television series. It had been a rough day so we were relaxing with a few drinks, just to unwind. I think maybe I had managed enough to pickle my brain because Graeme said to me that they were auditioning for the new series of the programme. In my stupor I just shouted, "Put me in for that, I'll show them what a cook is". Of course, it was tongue in cheek with no intention of it ever coming off.

I forgot all about it but Graeme and Linda had talked to each other when watching Ramsay swearing and directing his kitchen and Graeme had said, "Who does he remind you of?" That was the moment they decided to put my name forward.

It's true that my personality changes when I don my chef's whites. At that moment I become a Jekyll and Hyde character. When things go right, I am a regular Joe Public but the moment there is a problem, I get annoyed to the point of madness.

Things have to go right in a kitchen environment; I am a perfectionist about that. If it is a bad problem caused by someone's incompetent working, I'll tell them pretty quickly but once I've gotten my point across, it's all forgotten.

One afternoon, a few weeks later, I was driving in Teesside, which is about fifty miles South of Newcastle when I got a call from Linda. She asked me to meet her in a city hotel. My mind was working overtime and I thought she wanted to meet me for sex, food or drink and hopefully, all three.

As a married man, you relish times like that, when your wife asks you to meet her in a secretive fashion. It gets the excitement going inside and you just hope that it's what you expect.

The A19 is the road back to Newcastle from Cleveland and it's a terrible road. It's got a reputation for being a really dangerous route and all I could think of as I drove was the possible sexy evening to come.

It took me an hour to get back to Newcastle and find Linda at the meeting point she had given me outside the Imperial Hotel. It's quite funny because the Imperial was the first place I worked in a kitchen as a dishwasher on the black economy shall we say.

I asked her what on earth was so urgent, at which she pointed to the hotel and told me to go in as they were doing the Newcastle audition for Hell's Kitchen. She knew that if she had told me in advance, I wouldn't have come within ten miles of the place.

When I got inside, there were so many people just sitting or milling around. I was given a form to fill in and provided with a number. As I looked around, the others were all attending in suit and ties. I had turned up in a sleeveless bomber jacket and tracksuit bottoms. Not the best of starts.

The producers of the show were auditioning until 5pm and my number wasn't called until 4.40. When I arrived, I was given a questionnaire to fill in and I had a bit of a laugh answering the questions. I just put anything down on that paper and I would love to see it again now, it was probably the biggest load of crap ever written.

In all honesty, I thought it would be a nice experience but I held out no hope of going any further, so my attitude was quite blasé when I walked in. There were three producers sitting and the first thing I asked was what they wanted. I suppose I was quite brusque about it but that's me.

One of the first questions they asked me was 'why do you want to be on Hell's Kitchen' and I told them I didn't but my wife dragged me here. Then they asked me how would I feel if I was voted off the show first and how it might affect my business, Millers Catering? Linda told me to be myself so I said that my main fear was walking along in Newcastle and being pointed out by the Geordies saying, "There's that wanker who failed in Hell's Kitchen". That really was my biggest concern.

When I said the word, they all collapsed with laughter and I felt a lot easier. I knew then that I could be myself in the interview and that was a relief.

What I didn't know while I was in the room, was that Linda had been approached by the man introducing us to the interviewers, he told her that I had been in much longer than anyone else. That told Linda that I might have a good chance of passing the audition.

The interview was coming to a close. I got up to leave and

was asked if I could come back for an interview the following Friday. Amazingly, I said no. Linda and I were intending to visit London and it just came out that I couldn't attend.

When I got outside the door and told Linda, I realised what I had done. She almost killed me. As far as I was concerned, that was it, I'd blown it big style. It was lucky for me that the producers weren't going to take no for an answer.

We had made the trip to London and were standing in Harvey Nichols, looking at cookbooks on the following Friday. I really couldn't believe what happened next. In one of those coincidences that happen in life, I had just turned to Linda and asked her to imagine what it would be like if my face appeared on the book stand next year when my mobile phone started ringing. A year later, I appeared in the Hell's Kitchen book so in a way it came true.

As I answered it, a voice said it was the production office of Hell's Kitchen and they would like me to attend a further part of the selection process at Hammersmith College, on the Monday after the weekend. Despite me telling them that I was in London already and could attend right away, they told me that wasn't how it had to be done and to get to the college at the time stated. All expenses would be paid they said.

Despite my earlier reservations, I was now raring to go and wanted to be in Hell's Kitchen desperately. Just to bring me down to earth as the call ended, Linda told me that I had sounded too eager when I had offered to see them right away.

I broke out in a cold sweat and goose bumps. The excitement was unbelievable and I just wanted to tell the world that I was in the final audition for the programme.

We flew back to Newcastle that Saturday evening. On the plane, all I could think of was how I'd beaten most of those suits and ties to a place in the next stage and I felt quite proud of myself.

No matter how we tried, Linda couldn't get me a flight on Monday morning, which meant I had to fly back to London on the Sunday. It gave me just enough time to have something to eat and a sleep and then I was back in the air.

The hotel we had booked wasn't the most comfortable I have ever stayed in but it served its purpose. It didn't really matter much because I found it difficult to sleep, as I always do if I'm away from Linda. There's nothing like your own bed. I was up early the following day, heading for Hammersmith by tube. When I arrived, there were about forty others hanging around already. They were all winners from their individual areas, so they had done a great job of getting to this stage themselves. Apparently there were thousands looked at originally in the various regions.

We went through the questionnaire process yet again, filling them in was tedious but necessary I suppose. The producers arrived and the first thing they told us to do was to give ourselves a round of applause for getting this far.

We were split into groups of six each but for some reason our group had seven. I thought no more of it at the time but it came to be significant as things unfolded that day.

The instruction we received was to make a starter and main course out of the ingredients lying under cloths on the tables in front of our teams. We had half an hour to complete the task. I watched the others as they lifted the veils and began to discuss what to do with the food.

If I'm honest, our team weren't working as a unit so to get the job done, I decided to take the lead. Two or three cameramen were filming the cook off and were laughing when I just shouted, "Whoa, Whoa, stop, stop." I suppose the banging of my fist down on the work surface helped the dramatic tension. The reason I did it was because I could see us losing it all if someone didn't take charge.

I looked at one lad and asked him what a couple of things were on the table and he said a mango and some risotto so I just told them all we would have mango risotto as the starter. The other ingredients were a butter nut squash, some salmon and a portion of spinach. It was evident we could just cover the butternut squash with the salmon and place it all on a bed of spinach. It wasn't rocket science but no one was coming up with even the most basic of ideas.

When we had all worked out our varying tasks, the team got on with producing what we needed but one lad stood on his own cutting an onion into chunks. It wasn't in the plan for the dishes we were creating so I told him to hold on for a minute. You could see in his face that he wasn't happy at me pulling him up and he began to get really aggressive, poking me in the chest and asking who I thought I was and telling me nobody talked to him like that.

I think it was the moment that I grabbed him, when he thought better of his attitude. He continued to be aggressive though so I told him in no uncertain terms what would happen if he didn't change his manner. My blood was up and I was shouting at him, telling him he was a little arsehole and that he better get out of the kitchen now. He left.

As the situation calmed down, I realised that it was totally silent in the kitchen and everyone was looking at me. The cameras were all trained on me. I'll never forget looking at one of the producers' faces and the dazed expression etched there.

I can't be sure but later I thought that lad might have been purposely brought in to test my temper and reactions. If that was the case, he did his job well. When I asked the producers about him, they just told me to get on with my cooking but it was in the back of my mind that he might be waiting at the end of the cook off for another confrontation and it preoccupied my thoughts all through the session.

It wasn't that I was worried from a physical point of view. If he had been waiting to start something, I thought it might stop me from progressing on the show but I needn't have worried because he had seemed to have disappeared off the face of the earth and I was quite pleased about it.

When I got home, Linda was of the opinion that the incident had done me nothing but good, especially as it had been filmed. She thought they were bound to use something so controversial on the show.

At the end of the day, they had sent us all home and told us we would hear of their decision soon. It took them a fortnight to contact me again and I couldn't concentrate on work. My mind was bouncing between being convinced I had done well enough to be asked on to the show and in the next minute convinced the disturbance with the bloke at the cook off would stop me from getting through.

The incident with the lad had some bearing on my involvement in the show. The contestants had to go through a medical before they could appear but mine included a visit to the psychiatrist to check on my anger management issues.

It came to me afterwards that the producers had told Gary Rhodes that there was a nasty, mad Geordie coming onto the programme. By now of course, it's all over the T.V. and the newspapers about the show and they had asked Gary how he would cope if a contestant got violent with him.

It may not be apparent on television but Gary Rhodes is well fit. Every morning before he starts work he spends a lot of time in the gym, keeping trim so he told every one who asked that he could handle himself if the situation arose. He also has a right hand man, Andy, who is there to look after him and that man is a judo expert, nobody sane would have taken him on.

My appointment with the general doctor was a funny experience too. He asked me to strip off and lie on a couch which I did, thinking I was going to get a full physical but all he did was sound my heart. I've had lots of examinations by doctors before but I couldn't work out why I had to be naked just for that. I suppose he had his reasons but I have no idea to this day why I had to strip bare. He did detect a bit of raised blood pressure but told me that if I lost some weight in the two weeks up to the start of the show it should come down to an acceptable level and that was it, I was in.

It started to hit me then that I was about to appear in front of millions of people on the box, so my little insecurities started to kick in. Most people don't realise that I am a shy man inside and, like everybody else, there are those little demons in my soul, just sounding off and keeping my feet firmly on the ground.

At this point, the final ten contestants were asked what they would like to take into Hell's Kitchen with them and I'm sure the others asked for special knives or other cooking facilities but I was a little more basic than that. I asked for my guitar but they refused that, saying there may be copyright problems if I was playing live on the show in the dormitories.

The second thing I wanted was some good quality

deodorant as I told them I needed it if I was working with potentially smelly bastards. I am particular about my hygiene so this was important to me.

The next one creased them up especially, I asked for a toilet brush because I told them I wasn't putting my arse where someone I didn't know was going to squat. It sounds horrible and Linda keeps telling me I don't do my self any good when I say these things.

One other thing I wanted was long apron strings to go around my body. They may seem trivial but to me they were vital.

ITV had worked hard to get us into hotels where the press couldn't find us on the night before the show started. The hacks were hunting around as they do for the contestants in any reality programme but the company had done their job well. At least nobody bothered me.

Despite it being the first night and experiencing the excitement of the show starting, I was missing the family dreadfully. There's nothing like an impersonal hotel room with hours on your hands to make you think of things you're missing. I was stuck in that room with nothing to do except wait for the next morning. The television company had told me that I couldn't leave the room, so I ordered a good Geordie favourite, fish and chips, from room service.

My sense of smell is really powerful. It comes from a time on the Tarmac gangs when I got a bout of food poisoning from eating a pie which was off. In those days, I tended to bolt my food and I got the thing down in record time, then realised a nasty taste coming up.

One of the lads had broken his pie, showing me the contents and it was literally green in colour with the most revolting smell coming from inside it. From that day my nose has been foolproof in detecting food which is off.

As the waiter arrived with my order, I realised the moment I opened the door that something was wrong with the food. The good old nose was working once more. I took the meal in and the waiter left. Just to be sure I parted some of the fish and felt sick at the odour coming from it. Needless to say, it went straight in the bin. I honestly believe that if I had eaten that meal you would never have seen me on the show. On reflection, maybe I should have complained but being away from home was the most important thing on my mind. I simply reordered but this time a steak. There's far less danger of contamination with meat of that sort.

It was an altogether miserable night I spent in that place. My sleep patterns were already haywire and I was glad when the morning came and we could start the business of filming the programme.

It was an early call at five o'clock. The Hell's Kitchen people arrived to get me ready for the show, miking me up, taking my mobile phone, money and other personal items etc from me. Downstairs, there was a limousine waiting to ferry us to the location of the show which was a converted, derelict old brewery. As each of the contestants arrived, we were brought into Hell's Kitchen and met by the maitre d, Laura, who offered us a glass of Champagne.

That part you might have seen on the television, what you didn't know was that I was asked what I thought of the restaurant when I was there and I asked them what restaurant they were talking about. I know that you might find that difficult to believe when the whole thing was set out in its glory but as I walked along the red carpet with the cameraman before me, I didn't look around. My eyes were fixed forward and I hadn't noticed anything around me, just the people ahead, waiting to welcome me.

When you aren't a television professional, the whole thing is quite surreal so it wasn't any surprise that I missed a lot of what was happening that first hour or so. On a reality programme, you aren't given any schooling about what to expect, they want you to be as raw as possible because that's the best television for them, so you flounder a bit until you get used to being in an alien environment. Within an hour of arriving, they threw us into cooking our signature dishes with only forty minutes to produce them.

It's hard to describe how I coped with the stress of making that first dish for serving to a cook of the stature of Gary Rhodes, but my arse was certainly working overtime that morning and I'm sure I wasn't the only one feeling that way. Not only do you have to cook from minute one but you are in a kitchen setting you are totally unfamiliar with and have little or no idea where the tools to do the job are.

People still come up to me regularly and tell me how they enjoyed my first real scrap with Gary Rhodes. It might have been great telly but when I told him that I had prepared my King Prawn Rockafella from Cadbury's Smash, I thought he was going to burst. No wonder he bollocked me, if one of my own chefs had done that I would have thrown him out of the bloody kitchen, and if you're reading this lads, don't try anything similar.

It was an absolutely genuine defence when I told him I had done it because we only had limited time to prepare the dish but I don't think Gary was altogether convinced, he just ripped into me about the nerve I'd shown in serving instant mash to a chef of his importance. If I had a tail I would have slunk off at that point with it firmly between my legs.

Now you may not understand this, but I didn't think that Hell's Kitchen had started well for me after that, I can't think why.

The day progressed well but I was ready for the break we got at four in the afternoon. Each day we had an hour off at that time and I would take the opportunity to have a shower, while the others sat around and chatted.

Working in a kitchen is a sweaty environment so I just wanted to freshen up as often as I got the chance and that was at least three times a day. If there's one thing I can't stand when I'm working, it's a smelly chef with rampant B.O. Some of the others could have taken a leaf out of my book is all I'm saying here.

As I hit the sack that first night, I was exhausted, missing my family, had served a world renowned chef instant mashed potato and was in a strange bed, it was no wonder I thought the next day could only get better.

When you're thrown together with a number of strangers like we were on the programme there are some you will get on with and some you won't, that's just the way we are as human beings. In fairness, most of the others were fine. We did have our differences, which I'm sure came across on T.V. and I know I wasn't flavour of the month with Caroline for instance when we first started, but when she got to know me and what I'm like inside, I think she felt a lot more comfortable. She was from a much more privileged background than me and I suppose it was a culture shock to be thrown together with a basic Geordie whose habits include blinking and sniffing when under pressure but I'm sure that doesn't make me a bad person.

After that first day, we seemed to hit it off more. I quite liked Caroline if I'm honest. She was a lot more posh than I am but again that doesn't make her a bad person for all that. Unfortunately, Caroline was voted off the show first and I felt that she was very unlucky. There was no way on God's earth she was the worst cook but I think the popular vote went against her.

I'm always a bit suspicious of the more upper class people but Caroline showed me that there are good people in that group as in any other and I hope I did too. Aaron wasn't a bad lad who slept next to me in the dormitory. I just think he shot himself in the foot a bit by saying things about Gary Rhodes on camera and mike. He did do a cracking impression of the chef though and provided me with a lot of fun when he copied his character traits. Night times were like a fairy tale wonder with him. He would tell me bedtime stories and it would be kids stuff really but very funny.

One of the true stories he told me was about the time when he went for a job on Newsround. He thought it was the John Craven T.V. programme which used to appear on BBC, but in reality it was a newspaper delivery job. I was in absolute stitches with the way he told it.

Two of the others in the kitchen began picking on him and I stepped in to help him. It was the hatred of bullying which I've mentioned in the book before which overtook me and I just wasn't having it.

I just found Simon too demonstrative and when he sobbed after being voted off, it left me cold. Don't get me wrong, I had my tears a couple of times throughout the programme and I know it was highly pressured but I was always a bit suspicious of Simon's motives. He wasn't really my cup of tea shall we say. At the start of the programme, I really did make an effort to make friends with the lad but he was having none of it. There was no way we would ever have been bosom pals but I was happy to try and get on with him. Maybe he had different ideas from the start.

There was a moment on Hell's Kitchen which you might have seen when Simon is discussing things with Gary in the corridor about me and I come in after hearing my name mentioned a couple of times. At that point, Simon calls me a thug and things get a bit heated. It's a good job for him that it all happened on a T.V. programme because if he had said that to me in any other place or at any other time I would have gone even further in telling him what I thought of his childish antics.

In my opinion, Simon was a whinger, there was no doubt about that. I always felt that he resented me, probably because he had an inkling I might have a better chance of winning than he did. His animosity shone through like a beacon but we could have got along if he had only allowed it.

The biggest threat to me from a cooking point of view on the show was Sam. In my view she was an excellent cook and could have run me a close second, simply on preparing and making food.

She and I got on quite well until one point when I said something to her which she found very out of order. What it was is best left unsaid here but she had a real go at me on the show about it. When I think back, it might have been something I should have kept to myself but it was said in the heat of the moment and she pulled me up about it in no

195

uncertain terms. The trouble was that I started imitating violin playing as she got mad and that made the situation worse.

Over that eighteen-day period I lost over a stone in weight. It seems a lot but any chef will tell you that cooking is one of the most notorious professions for sheer hard graft and movement. You just never stop in a kitchen and the Hell's experience increased the levels of intensity five times. I am a big lad and I can afford to lose a bit but the work, late nights and early mornings just tired me out more than I ever have been in my life before.

There were other things which affected me too. Simon and Aaron really bonded straight away and I felt that they were talking about me and laughing at things I was doing. That got to me big time and I became a little paranoid about it. It was only my insecurities coming out and in a show like that, where you are closeted with a lot of people you don't know, it's great for working on your worries about yourself.

Things like that made me withdraw a bit. I know in the first few days of the show that I was becoming more and more of a loner and that's really hard to cope with. My broad Geordie accent was a stumbling block too. No one seemed to have a clue what I was talking about and it was bloody frustrating I can tell you. In my own mind, I knew I wasn't doing myself any good by distancing myself from the others in the red team, so I made the effort to try and blend in a bit more. It didn't seem to help, the others seemed determined to keep me on the fringe.

That hurt me a lot. As a bloke I'm a friendly animal and love getting on with people and those first few days were so tough to take. Gradually it got better but I don't think I was ever truly accepted by my team mates. They all seemed to be from the South of the country and we all know about the North-South divide.

Even Gary Rhodes pulled me one morning, telling me that I wasn't a team player. With all this going on, it wasn't surprising I finally snapped and in my one-to-one piece to camera, I told the nation exactly what I thought of the ignorance being shown by the members of the red team.

Actually, what I said was much, much worse than you saw on camera but it just couldn't be shown. It was one of the times that I was in tears on the show. If you think about it, I was away from my family for a long period and mine mean the world to me, I was out of my home routine and the ignorant attitude of those people was completely foreign to the warm, friendly Geordies I was used to. No wonder I broke down and told them exactly what I thought of them.

I still remember the moment I saw the dormitories and the flat upstairs for the first time. The production company must have spent a fortune on the place. We all just stared at the quality of the furnishings and the decoration. When you sat on the sofas you just melted into them and after a day in the kitchen it was difficult to pull yourself out of the soft cushions.

We laughed a bit at the Del Boy wallpaper as we called it but it fitted the general decoration perfectly. Everyone had a set of kitchen knives personalised with our names on them and so were the chefs' jackets. The bedrooms were equally fabulous. Male and female slept in the same dormitory. I don't know if Linda would have had that if she had known in advance, but it all worked out well.

As a bit of a joke, I told them I would have the bed next

to the door to protect everybody. In reality, it looked like the biggest and most comfortable one. As I pulled the covers back I noticed some suspicious white stains on the sheets, telling my team mates that they were there before I got in. They looked at me blankly but I wanted them to know it had nothing to do with me.

Scattered around the flat were lovely flower displays and being a keen gardener, I decided I would water them each day. There were a couple which must have been coming to the end of their lives and the flowers had wilted. The others were astonished when I showed them a trick I'd learned years before.

I took one of them and put the stem in some hot water, causing the whole thing to stand erect again, beware though, this only works on flowers. The others had never seen it done before and it gave them a bit of amusement for a few minutes.

At home I have a really lovely garden which gives me a lot of pleasure looking after it, so tending to the flowers in the Hell's Kitchen flat was a good bit of therapy for me during the show.

I couldn't help wondering who had slept in my bed on the celebrity version of the show, maybe Edwina Curry or Jennifer Ellison. I know which I would have preferred.

Granada Television was absolutely wonderful in looking after us from the first minute of the show. Nothing was too much trouble and even the smallest details got their full attention. When we finished each day in the kitchen and went upstairs to the dormitories, each of our bedrooms had bins provided with our names on them. All we had to do was drop our soiled whites in the bin and the next day they would be returned, laundered, ironed and bagged read for use. They also provided a blackboard in the main dormitory area so that we could mark up our choice of food for the end of the day. Whatever we wanted to eat would be provided, no matter what it was.

It caused a bit of humour one day when I asked for tongue. In the North you can buy sliced tongue in shops and it's a beautiful sandwich meat. I wasn't aware that Londoners don't have the same delicacy in the South and when I arrived on the evening there was a packet of full animal tongues in the fridge. The poor girl who had been given the task of getting my choice had scoured London looking for these tongues and God knows where she got them from. I think I opted for a cheese sandwich that day.

As I searched the fridge one night, I found a jar of peanut butter which was something I hadn't had since I was a kid. I just couldn't resist it and must have eaten the best part of a full jar that night. It gave me the taste for it again and I'm amazed that I didn't pile on the weight before the end of the show because of the amount I ate. It must have been all the hard, constant work which kept it off. That stuff is lethal but fantastic. The moment you taste it, you can't stop putting it in your mouth, it's that good.

You couldn't tell from the television pictures but the dormitories were up six flights of stairs from the kitchen area. It was a bind climbing those every day and sometimes you had to do that several times. The area from the kitchen up to the flat was pretty basic, nothing like the fantastic look of the living area. It was pretty dismal and depressing really.

At the end of the day, there would be interviews in the wine cellar which was down these stairs. If you were last to be interviewed it might be 1.30am before you got to bed. Going down for those talks always brought me back to the real world. They would mike us up and talk to us one-to-one, it made me feel really special and I really enjoyed those times a lot.

These treks up and down played havoc with your legs and a number of us began to notice broken veins in the limbs from this activity and being on our feet for eighteen hours a day, so Granada arranged for us to be provided with support stockings and that helped a lot. It was yet another example of the attention to detail the company provided. Putting those things on was like trying to get a football in a condom but the comfort they gave when on was outstanding. I will always have sympathy for ladies putting on tights now.

They had also supplied us with a type of clog to wear but I was sliding all over the place in them and I asked if I could have a pair of Doc Martins for the show and they provided a cracking pair. It was a hell of a lot more comfortable in them than the provided footwear.

While I was in the dormitories, there were many things which pissed me off greatly. Food was left lying around by all of us and we had flies buzzing around throughout the living area. I spoke to the others on a number of occasions and asked them to make sure there was no food residue on the surfaces but my moaning about it didn't seem to matter as it still went on.

The smoking aspect was another thing which got on my nerves. I've never liked the habit and most of them liked their cigarettes. There was the constant smell of tobacco in the dormitories, which penetrated your clothes and hung around in the air. For me, it was a difficult thing to come to terms with but I had to do it just for team harmony. In fairness, they all smoked outside on the patio area but the smoke still drifted into the flat when it was raining and they used to sit in the doorway.

Things which would never normally bother you, drive you wild when you're closeted in for days on end. Abby used to jog around the flat from seven every morning for a half hour, walkman in ears with that tinny racket pulsating out. I love music but it was driving me insane at that time of the morning. Mind you, the jogging made her look very fit and attractive. When you've had a hard day's graft the day before and little sleep you need a relaxing, quiet time when you first wake up. Abby wasn't giving me that. I kept quiet about it but it was hard to do. She was a really lovely lass and I really enjoyed watching the advert she did with David Beckham on television. I was relieved when she was voted off because I was looking forward to the peace in the mornings.

At the start of Hell's Kitchen we were told that there would be no contact with the outside world and there were many times that I missed Linda and the family very badly. If there had been any way of contacting them, I would have tried but Granada had made sure there was no paper, pens or any other things which might have been used to get in touch with your family or anyone else. It's true that you only fully realise what you've got in life when it isn't there.

Most of the frustrations I felt on the programme were as a direct result of being away from home. The cooking I could cope with, the loneliness was hard.

One evening on the show, I noticed a woman in the restaurant and told Gary Rhodes that it looked like Linda. It actually was her, GMTV had asked her to come for an interview on their show the next day and she was invited to eat in Hell's Kitchen the evening before filming.

Gary Rhodes and the producers gave me a few seconds to see her and it meant the world to me. I will always thank them for that.

I honestly had no hidden motives for being on the show. If it hadn't been for Linda and Graeme, I would never have auditioned for it but I'm sure a lot of the others were using the experience to try and get on in life. For that reason, a lot of petty jealousies and unfair strategies were used by some of the contestants and it sickened me to the stomach.

Aaron was one of them who didn't try to gain advantage by that sort of thing and I had a bit of a soft spot for him. He was a good looking bloke and he knew it. It was funny watching him preening himself in the mirror and combing his hair like the Fonz every day. It was obvious that the women would fall for him in a big way.

Kelly actually saved my life on one occasion. Someone had left the brat pan on in the kitchen causing the fire alarms to go off. I was in a particularly deep sleep, woke up with a start and then decided it wasn't bad enough to worry about, but Kelly knew better and dragged me out of my pit, luckily for me. She came back to get me when she could have just left the building so I owe her for that.

In fact, the incident was quite bad and part of the kitchen had to be cleaned up a bit. The pan had been blackened by the heat and smoke so it was swiftly replaced and the viewers never had any inkling about the seriousness of what had happened.

For the members of the show it was a bad night. None of us got any sleep for the rest of the dark hours and we looked like zombies the next day in the kitchen. At this point, the others decided they wanted to strike. I would never cross a picket line on a legitimate work dispute but this childish attitude really made them appear like prats so I told them to be their age and get on with it. Can you believe grown people would act in that way on a T.V. programme? It's quite sad.

Those dormitories had their moments and they weren't all savoury. On one occasion I had been stuffing my face after a period when I had eaten little and my gastric juices were working and I had a touch of wind through the night. My granny always told me, better out than in. We all do it but the others started to complain. Aaron had plenty to say to me until I told him that he must be a scenty arse and never did that sort of thing did he? He quietened down after that.

Shortly after that, one of the girls who shall remain nameless let one rip which made mine seem like a light breeze to her tornado. Of course everyone blamed me but I know to this day who it really was and I don't want anything for my silence.

In quiet dark rooms at night you hear all sorts of strange noises. There were plenty in that dormitory, I can vouch for that. It could be quite eerie when you woke up in an unfamiliar place and heard those sounds.

Jean Christophe appeared once in the flat after service. He would keep Kelly informed about what was going on in the show and on one occasion he sat with a few of us and tried to psyche me out, telling me I had no chance of winning and that Kelly was a much better chef and would win because of that. In the back of my mind, I knew what he was doing. I don't think he could believe it when I just said goodnight and went off to bed.

In fact, he was a very nice bloke and when Gary did his nut with me about the Rockafella with instant mashed potato, Jean Christophe made a point of telling me that he thought it was fantastic. He also told me how he felt for me being so far from home as he was feeling the same too. His style of cookery is much different to Gary Rhodes' and I would have loved to work with him for a while and pick up some tips from him.

There were all sorts of ploys going on between the contestants too. One evening after service, I was relaxing with one of the others, drinking wine and I noticed that she was pouring herself small glasses but filling mine almost to the brim. It may have been that she was being generous but a rival with a hangover next day would have been a bit of an advantage. Having said that, I prefer to think she was generous.

Alcohol featured prominently in the flat. We were given the opportunity to drink what we wanted. It was our choice and if we over indulged we would have to suffer the consequences. One night, a few of us stayed up and hit the wine quite heavily. The next morning we were in a bit of a state and I think it showed in our work, I know we all steered clear of a session like that again.

Every evening we were told to pack our bags in case we were the ones to be voted off the show next day and that was a depressing task. From the moment Caroline was voted off the show, I decided that I wouldn't pack mine. If I had been voted off, I wasn't bothered about picking up my gear. As far as I was concerned, the company could hold onto it until the end.

On my dresser, there was a picture of Linda and I made

the decision early that it would stay there until the moment of truth. She was the driving force behind me from the start and I wanted her with me until the very end.

I can still remember that first night when Caroline was voted off. Going back to the dormitory and sleeping there with one of the team gone was a strange experience. Everyone missed her and it brought home to you just how flimsy your stay could be.

It got worse and worse as time went on. One by one the others left and the last night when I was on my own gave me lots of time to think about the whole thing.

All I could think of was how Linda would kill me if I had managed to get that far and then blew it.

I'm sure I was the only one who didn't have any time off for illness or a treat throughout the whole show. Most of the others had minor ailments which kept them from service for a little while but I managed to stay on my feet for the whole show, which I'm quite proud of.

There was one moment on the show which depressed me more than any other. Gary Rhodes kissed me on the cheek once and I had no idea why he was doing that until he told me that Manchester United had beaten my beloved Newcastle in the semi-final of the FA Cup. He is a rampant red so it was particularly hard to take but I remember a certain 5-0 mauling we gave them at St. James' Park in the Kevin Keegan era so if you are reading this Gary, you haven't always had it your own way.

Whenever anyone was voted off, I felt for them. It must have been a horrible experience, which I was lucky enough not to have to go through. I related quite a lot to big Stein and I felt for him one night when he knew in his heart he would be the one to go.

As he was a builder and I had worked on the roads there was a little bit of a connection between us, so I made him a cup of tea and tried to console him. He was the closest personality to my own and I wanted him to know that someone felt for his situation. Maybe it helped, I don't know. You've got to remember that whoever got voted off by the public had still worked hard in that kitchen to make the whole programme work, so the shock of being the one to go must have been hard to take.

There were periods in the day when you had the most mundane jobs to do. One day, I spent eight hours shelling peas and the others had done similar jobs too, so when it came to that terrible moment when your name was called to leave, it must have been like a giant kick in the teeth.

I had gone into Hell's Kitchen with a blasé attitude but still felt terrified each time the voting process took place. Everyone's proud and feel they are the most worthy, which is natural. It just happened I was the one to get to the end and win but given other circumstances, it could have been so different.

Mistakes were made and I made one of the most awful of them all. Gary Rhodes had prepared some soup and had placed some tomatoes in a muslin bag hanging over a pan of what I thought was dirty water left by one of the others inside the fridge. I binned the lot and faced the wrath of Gary the next morning when I explained where his mixture had gone.

It was like a goldfish bowl in the kitchen area. At first I didn't know there were two-way mirrors around the walls and that was where the cameras were situated. There was a day when I splashed something up the mirror and smeared the glass when I wiped it over. When I recall those two-way mirrors I can remember checking myself out, inspecting my nose and it must have been a hideous sight for the cameramen on the other side looking out.

There were other chefs brought in to help us all out. They weren't really given any exposure on T.V. but I would like to thank them, they were magnificent in helping us achieve what we needed to do and if it hadn't been for them, the programme would never have been the success it turned out to be.

Adam was Gary Rhodes' sous chef and he really seemed to believe in me. He encouraged me all the way and his help to everyone was first class.

There are two people who were so helpful to me on the last night and I must mention them here. The first was the maitre d, Laura. All that night she kept telling me that the food going out was first class and that did wonders for my confidence. I want to particularly mention Lauren, the waitress. There was no chance to thank her personally after the service but everyone should know that she was fantastic for me on the night.

We came to the last night's service and I have never been so nervous in my life. Our former team mates were brought in to help out in the kitchen and Caroline turned out to be my rock. Aaron and Sam let me down by flirting with each other the whole night and this really annoyed me.

The night went by like a blur and I daresay we didn't do the best cooking of the programme's history. It wasn't surprising really as my mind was racing about the decision to come. Over the period of the show, I had worked my arse off to get to this point and to have it snatched away from me now wasn't worth thinking about. Everything depended on the great British public so my confidence was high that they would accurately reflect their true feelings. I wanted to win desperately but I had surpassed my wildest dreams just getting to the show. Whatever happened now, I could go back to Newcastle with my head held high.

They called us from the pass with Angus Deayton standing out front to announce the decision and, as I came out, I had the most dreadful of sensations. It was a mixture of nausea and light headedness, almost as if your blood pressure had plummeted.

I have watched loads of reality competitions on T.V. always thinking that the winner must have known in advance and that their reaction was staged but if any of them had the feelings I experienced coming out from behind that pass, they have my sympathy.

Deayton is a fabulous presenter with his laid back, wry attitude so his stretching out of the final decision was great telly for the masses but bloody awful stress for the contestants. I looked into his face to try and get a feeling for the judgement, only to see the bland expression he demonstrates so well.

Jean Christophe was standing behind Angus and took a look over his shoulder. His face went like thunder and he stalked off to talk to his sous chef, not appearing too happy.

At that moment I suspected I might have won but my natural instinct told me that I had been down roads like this in the past, only to be disappointed and my inner voice was telling me there was no chance that I had won it. I am not a massively religious man so when you saw my hand cover my face just before the announcement of the winner was made,

Rockafella

When I produced my signature dish for Hell's Kitchen, Gary Rhodes was flabbergasted that I had used instant mash potato. I have reproduced the recipe here and hope you enjoy making it.

Serves: 1
Preparation Time: 1 hour
Cooking Time: 8 mins

Ingredients:

**Piping bag of mashed
potato seasoned with
white pepper and salt,
cream and a little nutmeg
170g spinach
6 king prawns,
shelled and cleaned
1 shallot, finely diced
1/2 litre fish stock
Knob of butter
1 small garlic clove
5ml English mustard
15ml parmesan, grated
Tabasco sauce
Fresh tarragon
1 fresh lemon
100ml double cream
50g cheddar cheese, grated**

Method:

1. Boil the potatoes in salted water then drain. Make into mash potato by adding cream, butter and seasoning.
2. Put the spinach in boiling water for 10 seconds then cool in ice water.
3. Place the mash potato in a piping bag and pipe around edge of plate.
4. Place the spinach into 6 separate mounds on the plate.
5. Peel and clean the king prawns.
6. In a separate pan put a knob of butter and the garlic. Add the king prawns to seal them and then place onto the spinach mounds.
7. Add a drop of Tabasco sauce to each king prawn.
8. In a separate pan add a knob of butter and the finely diced shallots, cook until soft. Then add the mustard, fish stock, double cream, finely grated parmesan and fresh chopped tarragon.
9. Cover the prawns with this sauce and top with grated cheese. Place in the oven at 200 degrees C.

you might be surprised to know I was praying to God for the win and also that Linda wouldn't murder me if I lost.

When the word Terry was said, my emotions just poured out. Watch me and you will see the mixture of expressions on my face. All I could think of was finding Linda and Graeme for a hug before I took the walk up to be interviewed by Angus.

As Angus called my name out, Gary turned to hug me as the champion. Kelly grabbed me and started crying in my arms and although I wanted to celebrate with Gary, I couldn't let go of Kelly. I'd won but my heart really went out to her because I knew it could so easily have been me coming second so I really felt for the lass.

During the entire week, when I was interviewed in the wine cellar I had told the producers that if I won, I would shout for Linda in true Sylvester Stallone, Rocky 2 style. They seemed to think it was a good idea to keep us apart so that I could have my moment of triumph but in all the hype it went out of the window, sorry Linda.

Linda and Graeme were out of it too with emotion. None of us could believe we had done it. I say we because I will always be in their debt to my dying day for having the confidence in me to put me forward for Hell's Kitchen in the first place. It was as much their achievement as mine.

How I got through the interview with Angus Deayton, I will never know. The sense of adrenalin rush was phenomenal. I had never experienced that level of rush in all my life.

The party afterwards was something special too but I do remember sitting for a while on my own thinking, what happens next? Tomorrow it was back to the first day of the rest of my life.

There was one incident which sticks in my mind particularly about Hell's Kitchen. John McCririck the horse racing broadcaster arrived for dinner and was asked who he was backing for the show. He said Kelly. Being a fellow Newcastle supporter, I thought he might have given me the edge.

As you know, I am a big horse racing man myself and I watch John on the Morning Line on Channel Four every week. He never backs winners and voting against me just goes to prove that it was another bet he let slip away.

CHAPTER TWENTY ONE

COMING OUT

Hell's Kitchen was a very busy experience but no matter how rushed I felt, it never stopped me from missing wor lass and it made me think about everything I had at home and how much I missed it all.

The final interview I did with Angus Deayton on the show probably wasn't the best one done on the programme but all I wanted at that stage was to get Linda's view on my performance throughout its run.

As I sat down and looked in her eyes they told me I had done well but it seemed there was something wrong. She's a very strong person but the media had found out about Anthony being in prison and they had hounded her about it for the entire length of the show.

It got to her very badly when they were constantly knocking on my door, demanding interviews, all the time trying to lead her into a trap. It got so bad she nearly pulled me out of the show at the beginning of the second week. The longer I was in, the more the media badgered the life out of her.

At my initial interview for the programme, the producers questioned me about the kids and I told them that Graeme was living at home but Anthony was down the country. I told no lies about it and I think the production team thought he was at university.

The show was about me as a contestant, not about Anthony and why the press were hell bent on his story I have no idea. The lad is a category C prisoner, not a murderer or rapist. He got into a fight and paid the price for defending himself so the press intrusion had no bearing on me being in the show.

At the time, Linda was scrupulously honest and told the makers of the programme about the situation, although I'm not sure if they told Gary Rhodes about it. It's possible they did because he invited me into the outdoor area one day for a cup of tea and began talking about his kids. When he asked me about mine I kept quiet again. It isn't a pleasant subject and had no bearing on me or what I do. Although he looked at me strangely, I'm sure I made the right decision.

GMTV had invited us onto their morning programme the day after the show ended, to speak to the newspapers and London radio stations. Once again, they concentrated on Anthony's situation but I told them all that he was serving his punishment and that was all I was prepared to say about it. Even then they couldn't leave it and pushed me about whether Anthony would be working in my restaurant when it opened, "It would save me working eighty hours a week if he did", I told them and the moment I said it they were like a dog at broth.

I will tell you this honestly, I hope I never get into trouble with the law because there is no forgiveness whatsoever.

Granada provided us with a press officer to help with the attention and all the media commitments and I must have talked to fifty people that day, driving around London to the various press offices.

Our next step was the GMTV studios for our interview there. We were welcomed by Paul Ross as we arrived and my mam told me later that he had tipped me as the winner of Hell's Kitchen from the very first minute.

The producers offered us lunch, after which they came for me to go to make-up and I sat next to a guy who chatted to me for half an hour, wishing me all the luck in the world. He was a really nice Irish guy and we made our way to the studio together, sitting down on the familiar sofa. I was feeling daunted, this was the very first time I had appeared live on television.

It was a real treat to be interviewed by Phil and Fern, what genuinely nice people they are and I found out that Fern is married to a chef so there was a bit of a connection between us. As our spot ended, Fern said goodbye to everyone watching and introduced a singer named Daniel O'Donnell who was the bloke that had been sat next to me in make-up. He was great to watch live and very talented.

A few more interviews took place and before we knew it, we were winging our way back to the toon. After the time I had spent on the show, I was desperate to see my home and garden again. When I walked in a little bundle of black and white fur bounded towards me and there was little Tids, my cat, he was all over me. There's nothing like home.

Within two minutes of us arriving, the doorbell rang and a journalist stood there, clutching a stottie cake and bottle of brown, asking me what I could do with that. Linda told him to take it away because he was trying to take the piss and she wasn't having it.

The man looked a bit embarrassed when he told us his newspaper's hierarchy had put him up to it and in fairness he gave me a cracking write up in the following day's local paper.

As he left, I told him that I would have made a brown ale stottie rockafella out of his ingredients and he printed it in the paper, my mates had a good laugh about that. Things went quiet for a while after I got home so I got on with work and visited Anth regularly in jail. He told me that everyone in the prison had voted for me, the place going wild on the night I was announced as the winner.

Over the months, I was telephoned fairly regularly with offers for various bits of work or requests to open stores and businesses. It was really nice to be asked but I realised I was spending more time for other people than for myself. I really needed a little time to readjust to home life but as soon as the phone stopped ringing I missed it, that's how it goes I suppose.

Out of the blue one day Granada rang me and asked if I would be interested in appearing on 'Through the Keyhole' with Sir David Frost. He is one of my heroes and I wasn't going to miss that for the world. The trouble was that I had agreed to work with Gary Rhodes in his restaurant for four weeks but Granada told me that I didn't need to be at home when the filming there took place. It didn't bother me because I wanted to see how it came out live when I was with Sir David and the panel.

It was the perfect finale to a fantastic year as I headed to Granada's Manchester studios for the show. We were collected at the station and taken directly to the penthouse suite upstairs to make sure we didn't bump into the panellists who were Linda Barker, Juliet Morris and Anthony Worrall-Thompson.

As we settled in the penthouse I had a chance to talk to the other guests, Tom Avery and Alex Best. The last book I'd read was Scott of the Antarctic's adventures so Tom and I had a good chat about that.

I was a bit in awe of Alex Best who sat right next to me, she is a stunningly beautiful woman and then Amanda Wakely and Mica Paris came to the party. I made real idiot of myself by asking Mica Paris if she was still singing, not knowing she had a new album and single out just prior to the show.

A few hours later, it was my turn to go on stage and frightened wasn't the word for it, I was absolutely petrified when the others told me there was a studio audience of three hundred, it was a bit unnerving they said.

If you know the format of the show, you will realise that they show your house first and then the questioning by the panellists begin. When Anthony guessed who I was and knew my name, I was over the moon. As Sir David said, "Terry Miller, come through the keyhole", I could hardly breathe and it lasted twenty seconds or so until I calmed down but I remember saying to Linda that, if I never got another piece of television work, I had ended on the highest note possible by being interviewed by Sir David Frost. For me, he is the greatest television personality ever. When you consider he has interviewed so many great people including John Lennon and Richard Nixon, you realise you're in the presence of greatness.

At the end of the programme, Sir David took the time to have a really nice chat with me and Anthony Worrall-Thompson passed me his telephone number, telling me that if he could do anything for me, not to hesitate to ring him. I would have loved to appear on one of his programmes with him but I didn't have the bottle to pick up the phone and ring him, but that's the way I am.

CHAPTER TWENTY TWO

BUILDING THE EMPIRE

When I got back from Hell's Kitchen, the feelings of anti climax were pronounced. I had been a major part of a highly popular reality T.V. programme and now I had to adjust to life back at home and it turned out not to be so easy.

I found myself missing the limelight a bit and that was a real surprise. Having gone into Hell's Kitchen with no preconceptions and no thoughts of becoming well known, the resultant feelings of deflation got to me.

It had been a whirlwind time after I won the programme, with interviews on television and radio, but within days that all seemed to dry up. ITV had been as good as their word and the prize money was paid to me within days of the programme ending.

All I had to do now was decide about my new restaurant, find the premises, create a suitable establishment, employ the right staff and go forth into the rocky shoreline of catering for the general public. I think the television company were a bit concerned when they paid me the money because they asked if I was intending to open a new restaurant and I told them that I might just pay off my mortgage instead.

The search for premises began soon after I got back but it proved not to be an easy proposition finding the right location. Lots of alternatives came my way, including the offer of the top floor of the old Tyne Tees T.V. building on City Road in the town but that proved to be too difficult to convert to the kind of restaurant I wanted. I was grateful for the offer though. It's a fantastic building and well known in Newcastle, it just couldn't be utilised as I wanted it to be.

The publicity and support I had received from Newcastle was unbelievable and was much bigger than I could ever have imagined. It just goes to show how the wonderful people up here take to their own.

The popularity did get a bit overpowering, I couldn't go anywhere without people coming up and congratulating me. It was all nice stuff but very strange and I got a bit depressed at the goldfish bowl existence I had to lead.

We still had a restaurant to get underway and I searched high and low for the correct premises but nothing seemed right or was too expensive and it was getting me down. I must have had a hundred existing restaurants offered to me but not one satisfied the criteria I wanted.

Luckily, one of my near neighbours who ran a property business told me about a possible suitable building and we went to investigate it. The man who owned it wanted rid of it and it turned out to be perfect, right in the shadow of St. Nicholas' Cathedral and on a famous thoroughfare in Newcastle called Amen Corner. Some of you might remember a band by that name in the dim, distant past.

Originally, the building was owned by the man who has the bar next door and he had provisional plans to knock the two premises into one but that didn't happen so he put the building up for sale.

Finding the premises was just the start of our problems. We then had to go through the rigmarole of securing them. It takes time to deal with lawyers, accountants, government burocracy and the like and it's a minefield. You get one thing right only to find another ten things which are wrong.

Once we had secured the premises, the real work began. For a start the interior needed gutting and creating in the way Linda wanted it to look. She had fixed ideas about the layout, decoration etc and we spent months looking for the right furnishings, crockery, glassware and lighting to make the place look and feel different to the other restaurants in Newcastle.

I hadn't really known what to expect when we started the venture but within days I knew that it was going to take a hell of a lot of effort to get the place up to speed. One fixed idea I was determined to incorporate was an open pass. At that stage, I also decided that I would have a camera feed to a large T.V. screen in the reception/bar area so that the customers could see the food as it was cooked.

An open pass can cause a lot of problems when the pressure is on and diners can see the complications happening in the kitchen but I had decided that I didn't want to work behind four walls any more and I would rather people see a good working kitchen, which is more interesting than sitting bored at a table. We had every type of workmen imaginable, from joiners through to sanitary engineers ripping things down and building new facilities and to be honest I never thought it was all going to be finished. It seemed so big a job.

Graeme and I renovate houses and it was a difficult job trying not to interfere with the professionals as they went about their business. My particular involvement was the kitchen and I had some tremendous help from the fitters in that respect. They took on board all my needs and built a superb site for me.

It's really hard to imagine a finished restaurant during the building stage and the longer the building goes on, the less you can see the finished result. It all comes together over the last week I find.

Linda and I were having sleepless nights throughout the creation of Rockafella's. I had decided that the place had to be called that, it was just so logical after my success with the signature dish on Hell's Kitchen. My head was constantly filled with the problems arising out of the construction work. Even while asleep, I was dreaming of the damned place. Any little thing preoccupied my mind, making me as tired as I ever have been in life before.

Honestly speaking, there were many times when I wondered if the whole thing was such a good idea. It's brain fatigue which does that and now that we have the place up and running I wouldn't have missed the experience for the world but at that time, I could have easily thrown in the towel.

It affected us as a family. There was so much pressure heaped on our shoulders at that time, causing many arguments between Linda and myself. We had scheduled the opening and invited Gary Rhodes to open the restaurant and Alan Shearer was invited too so we had to finish the building work on time to fit in with schedules of these people.

When I won the prize on Hell's Kitchen, it was widely reported that it was £250,000 but it was provided as £200,000 cash, £30,000 of kitchen equipment and £20,000 of consultancy provided by Gary Rhodes. It was a hell of a good start but we still needed to find a substantial amount to get us underway. We needed to borrow to get us to the figure necessary but that's the way business goes round.

Borrowing is always a stressful thing but we had to go down the route if we wanted to build the dream so we took the chance and thankfully things went much better than we ever hoped.

Linda and I conducted the interviews fairly early to get the right staff and we had hundreds of applications. As far as the waiting staff was concerned, that was Linda's province and I stayed out of the picture for that part.

The kitchen staff was a different matter, that's where I come into my own. Having worked in London, where the culture is to make staff work every hour God sends, I didn't want that with my people. What I'm providing is a job, not a slave labour camp so I wanted my people to be happy in their work and have the time to enjoy life at the same time.

It takes time to get the right pegs for the right holes but I was really lucky to find a lot of good people from those first interviews. I can see them staying with me for a long time and I hope they do.

When we fitted out the premises, I wanted the kitchen to be as simple to run as could be with everything at hand as far as possible so that the workload is taken off the staff. That's where the kitchen fitment company were a godsend.

Each day as I visited the building site, I was torn between feelings of confidence and depression. Problems occurred constantly and most of them seemed to be insurmountable. The costs were rocketing as time went on, the right materials were hard to find and delays seemed to be a constant theme. It was a nightmare most of the time.

This was the first time that I didn't have to do the building work for premises myself and, in all honesty, I didn't have the time to do it. Looking at the place today, the builder did a fantastic job for us.

Linda's role is front of house in the restaurant and everything to do with the decoration of the reception area, bar, dining area etc was undertaken by her. She has a real flair for colour and style and she decided on a pale lilac for the main wall colour. It gives the place a relaxed and sophisticated look and people comment on its peacefulness all the time.

Linda wanted some different style tables and chairs and she sourced them from the internet. They came from Italy and are a unique style. We wanted the most comfortable chairs possible so she chose high backed ones and everything is in dark wood and that complements the decoration perfectly.

It wasn't easy to source exactly what we wanted, but we were prepared to search high and low until we got the right furniture items and it was the same with the crockery and cutlery.

Everything Linda picked for the table settings was the latest design with unusual plates, knives and forks etc. It just gives the restaurant that unusual feel and something different for the diner.

Hobart are the company who provided the kitchen equipment and they were the same company who had provided the kitchens for Hell's Kitchen. They're the best in the industry and if I was opening a restaurant, I wanted the best so we chose them for the equipment.

Every second you are constructing a new restaurant is fraught with problems but the only way to get to the end is to batter your way through the difficulties. Eventually though, the whole thing was finished and we heaved a massive sigh of relief.

The restaurant finally opened on the 7th December, 2005 and it was manic from the start. It's quietened off a bit now but it's still a very busy place.

It was very near Christmas and we had missed a lot of the pre-booked Christmas party trade but it was still massively popular.

At the same time we had the opening for the restaurant and that was a brilliant evening. Everyone turned up who had promised to be there. I know I go on about him but I was so grateful to Alan Shearer for turning up. The demands on his time must be enormous and to think he bothered himself to come to my opening meant everything in the world to me. He is the greatest footballer ever in my opinion and a real Geordie man. Newcastle United are going to be much poorer now that he has retired but I hope he comes back as manager one day because I think he would do a fabulous job.

A lot of the other Newcastle players turned up too. Shay Given, Lee Clark and a host of others and then there were my personal friends like Billy Hardy who is Julie's partner and Glen McCrory the boxer.

It had to be Gary Rhodes to open the place and the man was fantastic on the night. It's a great pity that we don't keep in touch now because he taught me so much over the period of Hell's Kitchen and he will always be my hero as a chef.

I'd like to mention too the other great people of Newcastle who attended that night. They showed me that I had touched something in the hearts of people in the North East. To everyone who came, I want to thank you for your support, it was much appreciated. Even the Sky television cameras turned up to film an interview with Mr Shearer and that was broadcast live from the restaurant so the viewing public got a great feel of the place from that.

All in all it was just a magical night for the family and me. It's probably something that will ever happen to us again but we have our memories of that fantastic night. True friends like my mate Darren and his wife Anna-Lee are very hard to come by. They arrived at four o'clock on the day of the opening and could see we were way behind time so Dazzler took over the bar and served drinks the whole night while Anna-Lee helped Linda in the restaurant area. You don't get many friends like that in this world, it's a bond only true friends have and they know how much I think of them for their help on the evening.

There was one unsavoury incident that night and I will never forgive the man who caused it. Linda had employed all the staff, bar one waiter who I took on for the opening. Throughout the evening he had been drinking which I was unaware of. Darren told me later that the bloke had told him he was my number two, so he thought it was OK to serve him.

I should have seen the problems coming when this waiter dropped a tray of twenty full wine glasses on the floor but I was preoccupied greeting and talking to guests so it didn't register.

At one point in the evening, the waiter asked if he could speak to Linda and me about something important and I invited him into the office but Linda was talking to Malcolm McDonald the old Newcastle United centre forward and I didn't want to take her away from a guest.

We got into the office and this man told me that one of our guests had asked two of the waitresses to have sex with him. They were Polish girls we had employed for the night.

He got really agitated while we talked, probably as a result of the alcohol and he was becoming very aggressive about the whole thing. He became more and more offensive and eventually I asked him to leave. The following day, I was visited by the police to say that he had made a complaint against me. Apparently he accused me of striking him.

I went to the police station to give a statement and tell them that nothing had happened. They understood the problems and no action was necessary but this person had taken a bit of the gloss off the whole night.

CHAPTER TWENTY THREE

ONE HELL OF A DAY

8 o'clock. The alarm goes off and I drag myself to the edge of the bed. Sitting with my eyes still closed, I can feel my feet throbbing from the night before. One hundred and five covers were served and I was on my feet for hours.

At the end of service, I sipped a few drinks to try and unwind from a stressful day and now my head feels like someone is battering a squash ball around inside it. It's that thick, horrible hangover feeling which stays with you all day.

My wife Linda has little sympathy; she had to put up with me babbling on about the whole night in the kitchen, instead of going straight to sleep when I got home. When will I ever learn?

The pain in my legs is almost too much to bear. It feels as though someone has been beating the backs of them with a stick and it's excruciating as I make my way to the shower.

As I pass my son Graham's room, who works with me at the restaurant, I don't hear any movement, meaning he is still asleep. It really pisses me off that I get up every morning and open the restaurant. Just once in a while it would be nice if he offered me the chance to lie in by opening it himself.

There's not a lot of time, so I push down a quick breakfast and leap (or more accurately crawl) into the car and race off to work. It's a busy day and there are many deliveries coming which I need to check.

I hope there are no police cars on the way because it's a good day for jumping lanes and being an amber gambler. Some people gesticulate and shout in my direction and I'm sure that it's good natured. The expression on their faces suggests otherwise.

As I pull up outside Rockafella's, my restaurant, I notice my staff standing around smoking like chimneys. It's something I hate to see with a passion but I have to put up with it. If I could stop them doing it I would but it's their life, or more correctly, their possible death. It astonishes me that people will put themselves in such dangers, knowing the potential result.

I'm beginning to get annoyed now as I notice one of the dishwashers and a chef are missing from the party, the outside waste bin is still full from the previous day and I'm wondering who you can rely on. There's no doubt the landlord will come down to complain and I am fuming. If there was a steam gauge on my forehead it would be registering in the red by now.

The problem is that they don't care enough about the job and that gets to me. I have done every mundane task associated with the kitchen, it was part of my training and I did it because it was expected of me, but these youngsters don't think they have to dirty their hands. I've got news for them, THEY DO.

As I finish dressing in my chef's whites, the butcher arrives. He's one who IS good and reliable and the four whole fillets, thirty supremes, eight packs of duck, bacon, black pudding and twenty pheasant are exactly as I ordered.

My first job is to trim the fillets and while I'm doing that the fish supplier arrives to drop his delivery of twenty monkfish, case of king prawns, box of mussels and box of oysters. The place is looking like a jobbing kitchen now and the smells are fantastic. The unfortunate thing is that the bloody KP and chef are bugging me in the head (a Geordie expression meaning I think unfavourably of them).

Don't let Gary Rhodes, Gordon Ramsay or any of those other celebrity chefs tell you any different, this is the way the catering industry is on a day-to-day basis and they have to put up with this kind of crap like anyone else.

The fish supplier has a touch of verbal diarrhoea this morning and wants to talk to me but I cut him dead, I'm just too busy.

As I work, I watch the other chefs doing their prep for the day, oblivious of the orders and that makes me lose my temper again. I tell them as I do each and every twenty-four hours to start putting the items away. Is it me or are simple instructions too difficult to understand?

Two of the waiters turn up. One of them just can't stop talking and I call her motor mouth. Her whining voice gets completely on my nerves and I'm even more annoyed at Graeme who lets her gob off all the time. That means I have to go and tell her to shut it and get on with her job.

I glance at the clock and see it's almost lunchtime. All I've managed to do so far is the meat and sort the fish. Where does the time go?

One of the commis chefs brings me the pheasants and I open the first one to notice a nasty stink. I ring my fowl supplier and tell him. His reaction is to tell me that pheasant always smell like that. It's probably not the best thing to say to me today so I tell him to go and boil his head. He sees it my way when I tell him that he had better get it sorted out or he won't be my supplier for much longer.

My wayward chef arrives to tell me he has missed his bus (not the most original excuse I've ever heard) so I tell him to get an earlier fucking one. He does this regularly twice a week but he is a good lad and I have a lot of time for him. I'm pleased when he does come in because lunch is upon us and customers are beginning to arrive.

I look around for my favourite chef's knife but it can't be found anywhere, so I look for Graeme. It's always him who takes it. If I've told him once, I've told him a thousand times not to cut lemons for the drinks with it.

He's nowhere to be found in the restaurant so I look in the bar next door and there he is smoking his head off. His face gives away the fact he knows something is up. He looks at me with the couldn't care less expression which he knows will kick me into a bad mood and I ask him where the knife is but he just denies he ever had it. I tell him he's a disgrace for a restaurant owner's son and storm out of the pub.

The first order is for pheasant (typical when there is a problem) so I tell the waiter to let the customer know that it isn't up to the quality required. The diner is understanding and orders duck instead.

There is yet another problem when the commis tells me that the rocket didn't arrive with the veg order and when I check the request sheet from the previous evening it's been missed off. The problem is it's an accompaniment for half the dishes on the menu, so I give the commis ten pounds, tell him to get his Seb Coe trainers on and bomb up to the Greenmarket to get some.

Lunch ends, we've served thirty and they've all left happy so now its time to clean down the kitchen and check the bookings for the evening.

I wanted to take an hour off but there's more chance of me playing for Liverpool. I'm behind and I need to catch up so rest is not an option. There's a stray bread bun and some cheese so I stuff it into my mouth while I contemplate what is still to be done.

Four chefs are hanging around so I ask them all what they need and it's a lot. There is the sweet chef, the chef de parti, sous chef and the commis and every one of them wants to go out for a fag. Amazingly, when I asked them at interview they all assured me that they didn't smoke. Despite the fact I don't like it, I let them go one by one. It's time to crash back into the fray once more and I start getting the sauces ready for the evening service. There's also fifty other things to make as accompaniments for the night time menu. It's 4.30pm and I realise I haven't even stopped for a piss, so I push a pint of water down to aid the flow a bit. It seems I'm dehydrated.

At this stage, I tell the lads to have a quick break but they say they aren't bothered and that they will work through.

I am rushed off my feet when two reps arrive but I'm rude and just tell them I haven't time to see them. I can tell by the looks on their faces that I'm not flavour of the month but it's tough shit. I have a restaurant to run and that comes first.

It's fifteen minutes until opening time so I slope off for a quick wash and put on some clean whites. A splash of Old

Spice and I'm feeling good as new.

I love this business and I shout "Are you ready team?" to the staff. They call back 'Yes chef' and the morale in the restaurant couldn't be bettered.

Almost immediately I realise that the fish supplier has brought frozen monkfish and undersized prawns. They are no good and I pull him up about it. He offers me discount but that isn't the point and I tell him that it's shit and I want them changed.

After eight hours of nothing but stress, my real day is starting. Other people are sitting in their cars on the way home, listening to Phil Collins and I'm just about ready to serve them when they hit the restaurant through the evening.

My first diners arrive and are vegetarians. I don't want to criticise but most chefs will tell you that they can be a bit of a pain.

The waiter arrives at the pass to tell me that one of the ladies does not eat fish, meat or any dairy product and asks me if there is anything I can recommend. I tell him a bowl of water and he is already on his way back to the customer before I manage to stop him to say, I'm joking. I look into his eyes and realise he was going to tell her that and I realise how frightening that is. You have to be so careful what you say in this business. To be fair he is foreign and probably didn't realise I was jesting.

She comes to the pass and explains that she doesn't want to be a pain but could I make a stuffed pepper with tarragon sauce and flagelot beans and she is happy.

It's only 6.30pm and the orders are coming in thick and fast. A very good sign this early in the evening and I'm already dealing with thirty covers. These are fairly simple checks from people just leaving work and mostly it's only a main course and dessert.

The service is going well when suddenly I splash myself with fat. From the pain I know it's a bad burn but I just don't have time to look. As the sous chef passes he confirms the seriousness of it.

By almost 8pm, the early rush is out of the way and it's quietened down. Like General Custer's last stand though, we know we are about to be massacred. There are forty people due by eight and I realise there are still seventy to eighty covers to be done in the evening. The fact is that they will almost all come at once.

My wife Linda has spread the bookings but Newcastle is a party city and when they get sucked into the atmosphere of the nightlife, people are nearly always late for their tables. I realise that I could do with a nice cooling pint like them and I note that I need something to refresh the parts other beers cannot reach but even a pint of Heineken is out of the question. After service I'll sink a couple but not just now. The shit has hit the fan and I've had about four arguments with the staff. I'll be pleased when it gets to end of service.

The people from the last check have disappeared into the night and I look around at the team. Everybody is sweating buckets and I shout to the waiter to get the boys that well-deserved pint.

We still have to clean down and it will all start again tomorrow morning but for now I'm proud of the lads and tell them so in my Geordie fashion. I still have to restock and do the orders for tomorrow's onslaught. It will be a hard one.

I'm absolutely knackered and I sink into an exhausted sleep at home. Suddenly through the night, Linda calls out and I wake with a start. She asks me what I think I'm doing as I've apparently pushed my fingers into her eye. It's then I realise I was dreaming of the service and it seems I was garnishing her face with lemon.

This business is going to send me round the bend but I would never give it up. Linda thinks so too. She tells me that I need a new chef's white jacket and to make sure this one has buckles and straps at the back.

AUTHOR'S AFTERWORD

If anyone had told me two years ago that I would be ghost writing the autobiography of a reality show winner I would have told them they were mad but as it's turned out, that is exactly what has happened.

I was working for a lifestyle magazine, in which we had published an article regarding Terry Miller. As I passed his new restaurant one morning, I was carrying a couple of spare copies of the magazine which contained the article and decided to pop in to give the man the magazines.

Terry happened to be standing next to the door as I walked in, taking the publications offered and asking me if I would like a cup of tea. That was my first encounter with the man and I knew from the first moment we met what kind of bloke I was dealing with, generous and friendly.

We began to talk, finding out we had a number of

subjects that we agreed upon. His opinions of life and injustice mirror my own to a great extent and this gentle giant's welcoming manner completely captivated me.

I had avidly watched his performance on Hell's Kitchen and could see immediately why the public had taken to him, what you see is what you get with Terry Miller. A man of passion, forthrightness and great warmth, he doesn't suffer fools gladly but will help anyone out he can, to me that is a real man.

Over tea, Terry told me he had long wanted to write his autobiography but though he knew what he wanted to write, he needed someone to interpret his words into a viable and logical account of his life.

I happened to mention that I had recently finished a novel which was with a publisher. It was at this point that Terry asked me if I would consider writing the autobiography as ghost writer on his behalf.

It's a very flattering thing to be asked to take on such a task, but my concern at that point surrounded the fact that I had walked in off the street and here was Terry offering me this opportunity so I mentioned my reservations.

We became firm friends within five minutes and he thought I could fulfil his requirements so I suggested that I take away some information and write it up as a guide for him, mainly to check style and he agreed.

My first effort was adequately written I thought but Terry was concerned that it didn't come across in the vein that everyone who knew him would recognise and he rightly wanted his book to accurately reveal his personality so it was back to the drawing board. Fortunately for me the second draft was more acceptable and we started from there.

Much midnight oil has been expended by both Terry and myself until we finally agreed on the version of the book you have just read. I have spent more time in Rockafella restaurant on an evening than I have with my wife and daughter for the last eight months but it has been well worth it.

Terry's generous nature in providing me with food has expanded my waist size to the point where none of my trousers fit me and I have an obsession about his chicken and bacon Rockafella. My mind is a whirl about Terry's cosmopolitan life too and I feel that I know more about him than most of my own family.

We've kept the Indian tea trade in business, judging by the vats of the stuff we have drunk.

Linda and Graeme have welcomed me into their home like one of the family, albeit a black sheep, and they have been extraordinarily patient with Terry and me on the occasions we have plucked away at guitar strings with songs that only we knew what we were playing Eric Clapton can sleep safe in his bed.

One of the most bizarre but pleasing things about the book was the moment when Alan Shearer rang me to provide the foreword for the book and I had just risen early morning when a voice said "Gordon...........Alan Shearer".

In my sleep induced state, I actually asked, "Who?" It's a very surreal thing to get a phone call from a legend but, like Terry, I would like to thank Alan for taking the time to help us with the foreword.

Over the months, I like to think Terry, his family and I have become stalwart friends, it's certainly the case where I'm concerned. The Miller family worked hard to make sure the book represented Terry in a true light and the fact that we have had a lot of laughs together along the way (as well as a few pints), has made the experience a happy one for me.

What I hope we have done over the course of the book is give an insight into a true Geordie, a warts and all account of the man and his struggles over his forty-seven years on this planet.

I would urge everyone to watch this space because Terry has plans to follow up this book with a number of other projects, which will have appeal to a wide range of readers and there are also some very important and high visibility plans that may come to fruition over the next few months in other mediums.

Terry Miller is a man who is constantly on the go, he never shirks work and his focus in life is to do the best for his family and his business. This is no plastic television personality. He's a man who will never forget his roots and will work hard till the day he dies and along the way he will make many friends through his sunny disposition and genuine feel for people.

As far as I'm concerned, I can't wait for the next collaboration between Terry and myself, the experience this time has been exceptional and I look forward to many long hours of friendship, beer and guitar playing in the future.